CHILLING TRUE TALES of OLD LANCASHIRE

Keith Johnson

Published by Sigma Leisure – an imprint of
Sigma Press, 1 South Oak Lane, Wilmslow, Cheshire SK9 6AR, England.

British Library Cataloguing in Publication Data
A CIP record for this book is available from the British Library.

ISBN: 1-85058-456-7

Typesetting and Design by: Sigma Press, Wilmslow, Cheshire.

Printed by: MFP Design & Print

Cover illustration: Kirkdale Gaol at the centre of 19th century justice – regularly visited by the executioners including William Calcraft (top) and James Billington (bottom).

Introduction

Before we indulge in these tales of Old Lancashire let us pause a while and consider the constitution of this ancient county. This was the Lancashire that had an extreme length of 85 miles and a breadth of 46 miles and lay between Westmorland, Cumberland, Yorkshire, Cheshire and the Irish Sea. The area of the ancient county was in excess of a million acres and as the nineteenth century drew to a close the population had soared to beyond four million people.

It was recognised as England's premier county in wealth, population and magnitude of business undertakings, being viewed by many as the workshop of the world. As life moved into the days of enlightenment and science groped her way through the gloom of ignorance, Lancashire had genius manifesting itself within its boundaries.

Great, for example, was the fame earned with its cotton trade and pride abounded as coal rightly held its place of honour. The county to some extent was the cradle of English railways and for inland traffic was regarded as the birthplace of the canal system. The coach roads had developed into the highways and by-ways necessary to support the factory system and the increasing engineering industries. Shipbuilding, iron and steel manufacture, glass production, chemicals, leather, pottery and numerous other trades were involved in the employment of the enterprising and hardworking folk of Lancashire.

The diversity of industry and commerce had been aided by the fact that the county had given birth to so many men of mark in different walks of life. Which other county could boast an Arkwright, Hargreaves, Crompton, Horrocks, Dalton, Roscoe, Whitworth or indeed a man to rival that distinguished politician William Ewart Gladstone.

Like all counties it had to endure growing pains with cotton riots, strikes and famines, yet the hardy folk shrugged off their tribulations and made their living with dogged determination.

It was a county that offered gainful and regular employment and attracted immigrants from far and wide. They came prepared to toil and sweat to earn their daily crust, content to eke a living working on the land, or in the mill, or even down the pit.

The county they inhabited was not a bright and gleaming one but a place with disease and pestilence. There was no welfare state to ease those on troubled times and health and medical provision was primitive in the extreme. The workhouse loomed large for those unable to cope and orphans and widows often suffered in silence.

Life had more than a fair share of accidents and atrocities and it is the tales of such that are contained within this book. Crime manifested itself amongst the poor who often trod the path of lawlessness to combat poverty and persecution.

The ale house had a prominent place amongst the lower classes and drink would lead to actions of remorse and regret. The parsons preached a moral code of Christian values, yet many poor folk forsook the path of righteousness and indulged in behaviour bound to lead to self destruction. The call of the conscience was often ignored and those who took to crime had to reap its consequences.

The justice system was a harsh and strict one and little sympathy was extended to those who transgressed. The police gradually increased their knowledge and their numbers and patrolled the streets and alleyways to give a feeling of security to the law abiding citizens.

The law enforcement officers were aided by the strict criminal code and what may now seem petty crime was often treated with tough and terrifying punishments.

Woeful was the offender who stood before the judges of the Assizes Court in Lancaster, Manchester or Liverpool, to hear the dreaded sentence imposed on them. The hangman was often called to administer the cold hand of justice and crowded transportation ships left these shores bound for the penal colonies.

The chapters that follow reveal the headline-making stories of the nineteenth century before Lancashire had Manchester and Merseyside snatched from its grasp.

The tales recall murder, mystery, mayhem and mortality amidst a bygone age and give an opportunity to judge the trials and tribulations of our county's ancestors. The events of these far gone days touched the hearts and souls of the county's inhabitants and reflect the hardships our forefathers had to endure.

Keith Johnson

Contents

Map of 'Old Lancashire' from a brochure published in the 1920s by Lancashire Industrial Development Council

Acknowledgments

I am indebted to the journalists of a bygone era who described the events that took place in great detail. The reporters of the following newspapers deserve praise for their accounts of the past:

Lancaster Daily Post
Lancaster Gazette
Liverpool Mercury
Liverpool Standard
Manchester Courier
Manchester Examiner
Manchester Guardian
Preston Chronicle
Preston Guardian
Preston Herald
Preston Pilot
Todmorden Advertiser

I further acknowledge the assistance given to me by the staff of the Harris Reference Library in Preston – they are quite wonderful.

Patricia Crook
My thanks to Pat who put her literary skills, time and cheerful encouragement at my disposal. I will remain forever grateful.

Glen Crook
My thanks are extended to Glen for his enthusiastic commitment to the book's photographic requirement.

J C Fielding
Once again I wish to thank J.C. Fielding for providing line drawings and sketches that accompany the various chapters.

Chapter 1

The Tailor who Cheated The Gallows

On Wednesday the 13th of August 1862, Walker Moore, a chubby-faced, stout little man appeared at Lancaster Assizes accused of the 'Wilful Murder' of his 32-year-old wife, Betty. The crime had taken place at Colne on the 5th of April of the same year and when charged, Walker Moore, a tailor by trade, pleaded 'Not guilty' in a firm tone.

The proceedings took place before Baron Wilde and gradually details of the couple's past and the incidents on the day of Betty Moore's death were recalled.

Betty Moore had left her parents home at Oakcliffe, in the township of Tothersdale, Yorkshire, when just seventeen and gone to live at Keighley. Shortly afterwards she married Walker Moore, who was some five years her elder and thus began a fifteen-year marriage that was far from harmonious. On a number of occasions she returned to the shelter of her father's house and each time her husband followed her and succeeded in persuading her to return home with him.

In February 1862, Betty Moore once again quarrelled with her marriage partner. They had not been living comfortably together, mainly because of his drinking which had reduced them in circumstances. She decided to flee from the husband who was not adverse to treating her with violence. Determined to make a new life for herself she persuaded her uncle Jacob Wood to employ her as housekeeper at the Hare and Hounds Public House, which he ran along with his son William Wood her cousin, at Black Lane Ends, Colne.

Settled into her new role she was somewhat perturbed when her husband arrived at the inn some six weeks later. With him was a man called Joseph Metcalfe and the pair seeking shelter for the night and money for their empty pockets, said they were on their way to a foot-race at Burnley the following afternoon. Betty Moore gave her husband a cool reception and although she gave him some silver and copper coins, she completely dismissed his suggestions that they spend the night together.

The two men were given a room for the night but Walker Moore was in a restless mood. He had a jealous nature and the comments of a young boy, who was sharing their room, that William Wood sometimes slept in a room with Betty Moore, added to his resentment.

During the night he consumed a quantity of ale and the following morning he was downstairs by five o'clock. Not long after his wife appeared and began her daily chores, in the house part of the inn.

When Metcalfe rose he was anxious that the pair should continue their journey to Burnley, but Moore insisted that they had plenty of time. With pints of ale and tots of whisky, Moore was content to sit and watch his wife at work.

Then as nine o'clock approached and Betty Moore was on her knees cleaning the fire-irons, Walker Moore left his seat and approached her from behind. Putting his left arm around her he raised his right-hand, which held a razor and ran it across her throat. At once the woman raised her apron to her neck in an attempt to stem the flow of blood which ran profusely from the wound. As she attempted to raise herself she staggered forward and William Wood, who had just entered the room, caught her and placed her on the long settle. Nothing could be done to save her and within five minutes she was dead.

As she lay dying Walker Moore went out into the road saying he would give himself up to the police. In his hand he had the blood stained razor and Wood and Metcalfe feared that he intended to end his life in a similar fashion to his wife's. Their fears were unfounded however, as he was soon back in the house and handing the razor over to Wood. He then moved over to his dead wife and leaning forward gently kissed her and said "she was a grand one".

Among the witnesses giving evidence in court was a local policeman who recalled that when he charged Walker Moore with the offence he remarked, "I came on purpose to do it". He also repeated other comments made by the accused which included, "I know she has been sleeping regularly with her cousin. It is all through her cousin and I would have been better satisfied if I had cut his throat too."

When the learned Judge summed up the evidence he remarked that the tragedy appeared to be the result of jealousy, but whether well founded he could not say. The law, he remarked, knew no immunity from the consequences of murder from whatever cause, and instructed the jury that if they believed the evidence it was plainly a case of wilful murder.

After a brief consultation the jury returned a verdict of guilty and His Lordship donned the black cap. Addressing the prisoner he remarked that he had with much deliberation and forethought taken a human life – one which he was most bound to protect. The sentence of death was then passed in the hushed court-room. When His Lordship had finished speaking Walker Moore leaned forward in the dock and said, "Thank you, my lord. I wish you would take it into consideration how you would feel if you had another man in bed with your wife". He was then removed and as he was descending the stairs, he turned round and said, "I hope it will be your case".

The execution of Walker Moore was fixed for noon on the 30th of August 1862. As was the rule the condemned man was never left alone from the time of sentence being passed and the morning fixed for his execution. Throughout the time there being always a warder of the gaol and a fellow prisoner in attendance upon him. He ate well and slept soundly, frequently talking of his approaching execution and saying, "He would meet his fate like a man".

The prison chaplain attended him daily and he paid great attention to his ministrations. On the Monday prior to his execution he was visited by a party of his friends, eleven in number consisting of two sisters, one brother, two nephews and three acquaintances, and some children. The interview under such solemn circumstances was most affecting and the condemned man was moved to tears. He had held out hope of a reprieve but the interview with his relatives dismissed that from his mind.

Not restricted to the prison diet he was allowed milk tea in the afternoon and for dinner generally a chop. He awoke usually at about five o'clock in the morning, but did not rise until seven. After breakfast he was conducted to the chapel, and the remainder of the day he spent in reading and various devotional exercises.

He complained very much of not being provided with Counsel for his trial, as from the fact that he had no money and had believed that professional assistance would have been provided for him.

On the morning appointed for the execution there was a large influx of people into Lancaster. Vast numbers of people had walked from Preston, Bolton, Colne and other places in East Lancashire to witness the last sad scene. During the night the highway from Preston to Lancaster had been used by a continued stream of pedestrians attracted by a morbid desire to see a man strangled.

William Calcraft, the executioner, arrived the night before and in his usual efficient manner he prepared the drop and made all the necessary arrangements.

The convicted man was said to have slept soundly on his final night and he woke about six o'clock. An hour later, along with a warder and another attendant, the pner was taken to the Chapel Yard for exercise. Moore was permitted to take his exercise in the Chapel Yard, rather than the traditional exercise area, because it afforded greater privacy, not being overlooked by windows of prison cells.

After some ten minutes he requested permission to visit the water closet he had been in the habit of using. There were three water closets in the Chapel Yard, and all of them were provided with water for flushing from a large leaden tank that ran the length of the three cubicles. A couple of minutes after Moore entered the closet the warden addressed a remark to the prisoner but got no reply. Sensing something was amiss he opened the door and found the prisoner missing.

The two men realised instantly that Walker Moore had climbed up into the cistern tank. There was a ledge just above the toilet seat and it appeared that he had used this to clamber up into the tank which was some five feet square and fifteen feet long. One of the men instantly raised the alarm and the other went in pursuit of the condemned man. With difficulty he raised himself up to the level of the tank which had some four foot depth of water in it and observed Walker Moore beneath the water line.

Hangman William Calcraft had a wasted journey

After a great deal of effort Walker Moore was removed from the cistern tank and the resident surgeon who was in attendance attempted to revive him. Around the convicts neck was a handkerchief which had been tied very tightly with a running noose. Nothing could be done to restore any sign of life and the convicted wife killer was declared dead from a combination of strangulation and suffocation.

When news of Walker Moore's suicide reached the ever increasing crowds they very loudly expressed their disappointment. The prison officials were stunned by the convict's action and the general opinion was that he had shown no sign to indicate he would attempt to cheat the gallows. The inquest into his unusual end was held the same afternoon and the jury returned a verdict that, Walker Moore committed suicide being at the time in a sound state of mind.

His body was interred a little before midnight in the presence of about a thousand spectators, many of them females. A strong body of the county and borough police were there to keep order and no disturbance took place. On account of his being a 'felo-de-se' no burial service was read over his grave.

Postscript: Towards the end of October 1862, the residents of Lancaster were once again stunned when it was revealed that another suicide had taken place at Lancaster Castle. The man concerned was Richard Threlfall who was on remand for assaulting his wife. The cell in which he was confined was considered one of the safest in the castle. The warder, as was his custom, went round the various cells to see that all the gas lights were extinguished. On looking through a spy hole into the cell in which Richard Threlfall was confined, he noticed the gas was burning, but was unable to see the prisoner. Entering the cell the warder was faced with the terrible sight of Threlfall suspended by his neck from the gas pipe that ran along one of the walls. He had prised a portion of the piping sufficiently far from the wall to enable him to draw his pocket handkerchief through and form a kind of noose. Then he had joined this to his neckerchief which was round his neck, by means of a slip knot. The latter he had done while positioned on a ledge, and finally he had jumped off the ledge and strangled himself.

No blame was attached to any of the officials of the gaol, and when the inquest was held the jury returned a verdict of "Suicide from temporary insanity".

Chapter 2

Sad Sequel to a Case of Typhoid

In November 1875, in the quiet village of Bispham Green, Mawdsley, near Rufford lived the Christopher family. Their place of abode was one of the cottages known as "Clark's Cottages". Thomas Christopher, aged 23, was employed as a horseman by William Clark, whose extensive farm buildings lay close by. For close on five years Thomas Christopher had been so employed and along with his wife Mary, aged 25, and three children, William aged 4, Margaret aged 2½ and Jane an eight-month-old baby, they had led a pleasant enough existence.

That November Thomas Christopher who was a steady, industrious fellow, caught a very severe cold which after a few days rendered him unfit for work. His wife who was described as a decent and quiet woman, dutifully nursed him along but his condition got no better. Eventually, a week before Christmas it was decided that the local doctor should be called and his visit diagnosed the sick man as having contracted typhoid fever.

The gravity of her husband's condition terrified the wife, who dreaded the thought of being bereft of her partner. She continued to administer what comfort she could to him and was supported by neighbours and relatives.

Finally on the evening of Tuesday, December 21st, the sick man's condition began to deteriorate rapidly. Throughout the night Mary Christopher and the sick man's brother, William Christopher, remained at his side to provide the constant attention he needed. Life was fast ebbing away and as the clock struck five, Thomas Christopher breathed his last.

The brother left the house soon after to inform others of the sad event, leaving Mary Christopher alone with her three children. Less than an hour later, the deceased man's brother returned to the cottage along with a couple of neighbours and the sight that greeted him was one of a horrifying nature.

On entering the kitchen he saw Mary Christopher crouched on the floor with her head resting against a bed that was in the kitchen, and on the bed were the three children all laid down, frothing at the mouth and obviously in great agony. There was a dark discolouration around their mouths and partly on their cheeks, and their appearance was all the more fearful by scratches which had been caused either by their scratching their faces owing to the burning effect of the fluid which had been forced upon them, or by the resistance they offered to taking the dose of poison which had been administered.

The woman was struggling in the throes of death and appeared to be in an insensible condition, while the children were having difficulty in breathing. Both medical assistance and the local constabulary were immediately informed and by six o'clock PC Drabble, from Rufford, was at the scene. By then the woman was dead and the constable noticed by her side a bottle of carbolic acid and a cup which had in it a measure of the deadly liquid.

Soon after Dr Dandy, who had been attending to the dead man, arrived and he immediately diagnosed that the children were suffering from the effects of taking carbolic acid. He at once administered what medical aid he could and the children were removed to the nearby home of their grandfather. The two elder children began to respond to the treatment, but for baby Jane little could be done. Eventually on Friday morning, which was Christmas Eve, she died to bring more sorrow to the tragic family.

Not surprisingly the awful affair threw a gloom over the entire district that Christmas in 1875, and the residents of the locality could hardly believe that such a fearful episode could have been enacted within their midst.

The inquest on the bodies of Mary Christopher and Jane Christopher was held at the Eagle and Child public house in Bispham Green and great interest was generated in the proceedings.

The sad events surrounding the deaths were related to the coroner and great emphasis was placed on the condition of the dead woman. It was related how fearful she had been of her husband's imminent departure from this life. Her brother-in-law stated how he had tried to reassure her of support from the family and that he had told her, "not to worry as you will be provided for".

A neighbour, Mary Yates who had been a constant source of support for the deceased woman, told the coroner that on the Tuesday afternoon Mary Christopher had said to her, "I'll make myself and the children away if anything happens to him". She had not however taken the threat seriously, feeling that it was only the reaction of a distraught woman.

She then went on to relate to the inquest Mary Christopher's words to her as she lay dying the following morning. Pointing to the bottle of carbolic acid and the cup she had said, "I have done what I said I would do". The carbolic acid was at hand because it had been used for disinfecting purposes during the time that her husband had been suffering from the fever.

Inside the Eagle and Child Inn, Bispham Green, the coroner was told of Mary Christopher's fears

When all the evidence had finally been given, the coroner stated that it was absolutely clear that the poor woman had died from the effects of taking carbolic acid and that the baby had died from the same cause. He then pointed out to the jury that if the woman had taken the poisonous substance knowing it to have been poisonous, with the deliberate intention of putting an end to her life, then provided she was of a sound state of mind it was their duty to return a verdict of felo-de-se.

Regarding the child, the coroner emphasised that if the poison had been given to the child with the intention of making away with her life also, then Mary Christopher would be guilty of wilful murder in that instance.

The coroner told the jury that they must consider the deceased woman's state of mind at the time, and the fact that her husband's death had occurred a short time before, a death that she was most apprehensive about.

The room was then cleared for a few minutes in order that the jury might deliberate their verdict. When the reporters were re-admitted, the Foreman of the jury announced that the jury did not find that the woman was deranged when she committed the act.

The coroner then replying that there would be no alternative but to return a verdict of felo-de-se against Mary Christopher and a verdict of "Wilful Murder" in the case of the child.

It was a sad ending to a tragic case and later when details of her family's history were revealed, there was much sympathy for Mary Christopher. It was related how the father of the unfortunate woman had been a hay dealer residing at Croston, and that he had been caught between the buffers of a railway wagon at Liverpool Station at the time of the Crimean War, and had died shortly afterwards. Her mother had also been killed on the railway and her grandmother who lived at Manchester, and had brought up the girl, was at the time of the tragedy lying on her death bed.

Chapter 3

A Stalker Strikes on a Foggy Morn

At around half past seven in the morning on the 10th of November 1890, Elizabeth Jane Holt left her home in Egerton, which she shared with her widowed mother and a sister, and set off for Belmont where she was employed as a schoolmistress. It was her custom on a Monday morning to walk the three or four miles to Belmont where she would stay until her scholastic duties were complete on the following Friday or Saturday.

The road she travelled passed by a steep declivity, with only a farm house here and there standing back in the fields. The morning was a foggy one with drizzling rain and, as the 21-year-old hurried on her way, she was seen on the Longworth road by several farmers who were on their way to town with milk. Those who saw her also noticed that following in her wake was a man called Thomas Macdonald, aged 37.

Macdonald, who also lived in the neighbourhood, was a man with an unenviable past, having been charged as a teenager with a criminal assault on a girl of nine, and in 1882 having been sentenced to 10 years penal servitude for a similar offence. In February of 1890 he had been released from prison on a ticket of leave and returned to the district to live with an aunt who earned her living as a mill operative. Since his return, Macdonald's reputation had not been improved by his actions and when a man named Mather was found drowned it was suspected, but not proved, that Macdonald was the cause of his death.

The auburn haired Miss Holt, who was of amiable temper and well liked in the district, had to pass the house where Macdonald lodged on her way to Belmont, and she had confided in friends that she was fearful of him.

That Monday morning Miss Holt never reached her destination, but her absence from school did not cause any alarm with Mr Swales, the schoolmaster, believing that she was sick. On the other hand, her mother and sister were of the opinion that she had reached Belmont as usual and was at her lodgings.

No inquiry was made and it was not until the following Saturday

Schoolmistress Miss Holt never reached her destination

morning that the mother and sister became anxious. When she had not arrived home on the Friday afternoon it was thought she had determined to stay until the Saturday, as on previous occasions. At noon on the Saturday, at the mother's request, a young fellow rode over to Belmont on his bicycle and learned for the first time that Miss Holt had not been to school at all that week.

A search was at once begun and when a young son of a farmer at Longworth Hall heard of the disappearance he told his parents that a couple of days earlier, while out with the dog, he had noticed an umbrella in the area known as "the wood". Acting on this information his elder brother went to the spot and found the umbrella. A little further down the ravine he observed evidence of a struggle and saw a track through the long grass as if something had been dragged along. As he followed the trail he noticed strewn about the place, a packet of tea and coffee, some butter in a paper, buttons off a woman's cloak, a hat and a pair of slippers. The trail continued on a steep decline and when the lad reached an overhanging crag he saw a pile of dead leaves and ferns. Beneath the mound lay the body of Miss Holt in a recumbent position, with her clothing literally torn off her back. Her jacket was ripped away from about her body and her corsets were laid alongside her. Her throat had been cut from right to left, the gash being deep and reaching almost from ear to ear. Her wrists bore evidence of having been fiercely held and there were slight abrasions about the face and body. Along the trail were found buttons torn off the girl's attire and from the appearance, her killer must have dragged her down feet first.

The police had been busy making enquiries and at eight o'clock that night, four hours after the body was discovered, Thomas Macdonald was arrested at his lodgings. He made no reply to the charge and seemed quite indifferent when placed in a cell.

Several witnesses had come forward and were only too willing to confirm Macdonald's presence on the road to Belmont on the previous Monday morning. That same day Macdonald had got drunk and was locked up, being later bailed out. A sum of eight shillings, which the girl had with her when she left home, was missing and the prisoner, who had followed no employment for some time, had been very free with his money on the Monday afternoon in the Black Lion beer-house, in Turton Street. Others told of the fact that his clothes had been bloodstained that day and on examination his pocket knife revealed stains upon it.

When the inquest was held at the Police Court the evidence pointed so conclusively to Macdonald that he volunteered a confession. In it he claimed that he had overtaken Miss Holt on the highway and accused her of spreading lies about his behaviour. He said that when she had denied the remarks and refused to retract the comments he flew into a rage and, after knocking her to the ground, he cut her throat. According to Macdonald he then dragged her body down the ravine and covered it with fern fronds and oak leaves.

Regarding the disarranged clothing, he stated that he had torn them apart to check if her heart was beating. He then denied that he had violated the girl or that he had taken her purse or its contents. The confession was not credited in official quarters as it seemed to be dictated by the hope of reducing the capital charge to one of manslaughter.

A medical examination of the body of the poor girl led to a report in which the doctor said her skull had been battered and smashed in a sickening fashion.

Although much of the evidence at the trial was of a circumstantial nature the verdict was one of Guilty and Macdonald was sentenced to be hung. The condemned man knew that the crime he was convicted of had created such a feeling of horror that no degree of sympathy would be shown.

Macdonald's execution was set for the 30th of December at Kirkdale Gaol and on the previous day he was allowed a visit from his aunt, Honor Bann and a cousin. The visit lasted for about fifty minutes and was conducted in the presence of three warders. There was a thick iron grating between the condemned man and his visitors and during the interview he acknowledged the justice of his sentence saying, "I deserve all I am going to get in the morning".

The aunt was painfully affected by the situation and broke down with Macdonald also weeping as the visit ended. As his aunt departed he repeated over and over again, "Good bye, Aunt Honor, and God Bless you".

That night James Berry, the executioner, arrived at the gaol and immediately went to inspect the gallows. His examination was minute, owing to the fact that new apparatus was to be used. The new gallows incorporated a link chain attached to the cross beam. The noose to go round the murderer's neck was of the same hempen material as previously used, this being fastened into an eyelet in the link chain and secured with a pin.

Berry seemed satisfied with the arrangements after repeated experiments with weights. As the gallows stood, the crossbeam was 12 feet from the trapdoor and the pit below was 12 feet deep.

On leaving the gaol Berry booked into a nearby hotel and ordered supper before he retired. Word of his arrival soon spread and a curious crowd gathered to observe his every move.

Macdonald retired to rest shortly after ten o'clock and he slept fitfully and restlessly until six o'clock in the morning, when he was aroused to receive a visit from the Roman Catholic chaplain. Half an hour later the condemned man attended Mass in the chapel and received Holy Communion. Upon returning to the condemned cell he was served with breakfast. This consisted of tea, toast and eggs which he ate with relish.

Some ten minutes before eight o'clock Macdonald was escorted from his cell to a building a few yards from the scaffold. He walked with perfect steadiness and appeared remarkably calm. Once inside the building he was pinioned by Berry and by the appointed hour he stood upon the scaffold. Berry wasted no time in fixing the noose and as the chaplain uttered the words, "Lord, have mercy upon me", the lever was drawn. Death appeared to occur instantly and there was not the slightest vibration of the rope. The executioner had allowed the convict a drop of 9ft 2in and it was subsequently found that the rope had stretched 13 inches. Macdonald's weight was 8st 12lb which indicated that during his incarceration he had lost close upon a stone.

On a cold morning with a biting east wind, and a slight fall of snow, only a small crowd had gathered outside the gaol and shortly after eight o'clock they witnessed the raising of the black canvas which was soon fluttering in the breeze.

Ten minutes later a messenger from a local hotel arrived at the gaol carrying a large tray covered with a white napkin. It was Berry's breakfast and the messenger remarked that the hangman fairly needed a good feed after such a gruesome task.

Kirkdale Gaol, scene of Macdonald's execution.

Chapter 4

The Jealous Lodger's Axe Attack

The goings-on at a lodging house in Burnley in the summer of 1894 were to occupy the thoughts of the town's residents for a considerable time. The house that was to attract such attention was in Lomas Street, off Sandy Gate. It was run by Mrs Mary Ann Allen who was separated from her husband and who earned her living by taking in lodgers and doing washing.

In the house lived Mrs Allen, her daughter Mrs Robinson, William Crossley, Adam Robinson, Robert Chadwick and his two children. William Crossley, a foundry labourer who also worked part time at the nearby Waterloo Inn, had lived at the house for about 12 months. During his period at the house Crossley became friendly with Mrs Allen and the couple began to cohabit. Their relationship did not run smoothly and Crossley started to grow jealous of Mrs Allen's attention towards another lodger. Matters began to become strained in June of that year and the landlady decided it would be best if Crossley found alternative accommodation.

On the morning of Monday, June 11th, Crossley's bags were packed for him and it was requested he leave that evening. That morning he went to the Globe Ironworks as usual and while packing some looms, he remarked to a colleague that he had a job on at lunchtime and if it came off he should not come back any more.

At mid-day when Crossley arrived back at the lodging house the lodgers and the family were at the dining table. He did not speak on entering, but went down into the cellar and brought out an axe. Then, as Mrs Allen was in the act of drying her hands on the towel behind the kitchen door, he struck her a fearful blow and she fell to the ground. As he prepared to deliver a second blow he was stopped by Robert Chadwick who, with the aid of Adam Robinson and the landlady's daughter, attempted to disarm him. They were unable to do so and the latter two received dangerous blows to the head in the subsequent struggle. The other residents ran into the street to raise the alarm.

His dreadful deed performed, Crossley left the lodging house and shortly after appeared in the public house that he often frequented.

Killer William Crossley entered the Waterloo Inn at Burnley (Glen Crook)

Conversing with the landlord he admitted his terrible actions and when the proprietor questioned his tale he said, "I have an' all. I shall have to be hung, and I'll die like a man".

Going to the front door of the public house the landlord saw crowds of people heading towards the scene of the crime. Catching the attention of a constable he notified him of Crossley's presence at the inn and the fugitive was immediately apprehended.

When the police were removing him from the hotel to a cab, Crossley waved his arms to the crowd and began singing, "Ta-ra-ra-boom-de-ay", and pointing to a lamp post he said, "You might as well hang me up on that and have done with me at once". When entering the police station he showed the same bravado and seemed in a hilarious and garrulous state of mind.

The blow to 56-year-old Mrs Allen had led to her almost immediate death and at the time of the coroners inquest her daughter was too badly hurt to appear, whilst Adam Robinson appeared with his head wounds bandaged.

It was recounted there that Crossley was only charged with the capital offence some six hours after his arrest due to the fact that he was initially in a state of extreme excitement.

Reviewing the evidence produced, the verdict of the coroners court was one of "Wilful Murder" and the feeling was that it was a premeditated action.

The subsequent trial confirmed the inquest's findings and 43-year-old Crossley was sentenced to be executed for the murder of the 56-year-old mother of three grown up children.

Crossley was described as a man who was remarkable for his honesty and harmlessness by those who had known him in better days. He was said to be a man who "could not stand corn" and one who, if he had a shilling in his pocket, must spend it. For eight years he had been a bar man and general servant at the local public house. It was said that in his time he had chopped up more firewood than any other man in Burnley. Those who had employed him all testified as to his good qualities.

At the end of July 1894, came Crossley's final day of reckoning. During the closing hours of his life he displayed none of the bravado which had characterised him during his trial, and he attended to his ministrations with the chaplain with much earnestness.

He did not express any sorrow for his crime and in an interview with his brother he remarked, "I've done the deed and do not rue it".

The executioner was the slightly built James Billington, who hailed from Farnworth, near Bolton and he expeditiously carried out the requirement of the law within the precincts of Strangeways Gaol. Crossley who weighed upwards of 14 stone had a short drop and after a slight movement of the rope, all was still.

A party of friends of the culprit walked from Burnley to Manchester to be present in the vicinity of the gaol during the execution. The black flag was kept hoisted for one hour, and the body was then cut down and removed to the mortuary.

Chapter 5

No Air to Breathe

The revolution in the iron industry led to the development of the coal fields, in which Britain was found to be singularly rich with vast mining undertakings in the Midlands, South Yorkshire, South Wales, the Tyne, the Clyde and South Lancashire. From time to time the coalfields were the scene of terrible catastrophes and scores of miners were swept into eternity.

Such an occasion was the last Thursday in November in the year 1868. On that day an accident occurred at the Springs Colliery at Hindley Green, some three miles from Wigan, that ranked amongst the most terrible mining disasters ever to have taken place.

The pit, situated about half a mile from Hindley Green railway station, had been sunk about four years and the shaft descended to the rich but fiery Arley mine, about 300 yards below the earth's surface. There were few, if any, old workings to embarrass the engineers and the seam, according to those qualified to judge, was as near perfect as possible.

On the fatal day the firemen made their customary inspection at six o'clock in the morning and reported that the state of the pit was perfectly satisfactory. In consequence the miners descended to their labours with confidence. From the pit eye the workings extended in two directions – to the east where 150 men took up employment and to the west, where the remainder of the 250 miners were digging. All was apparently well until half past eight o'clock that morning when a terrific explosion took place in the west seam, an explosion so loud that it could be heard a mile away.

The first news of the disaster was relayed by an underlooker named Drinnan, who was close to the outlet shaft at the time. He arrived at the surface on a load of full tubs and told the manager, Thomas Southworth, of the devastation down below.

At once an active band of volunteers descended to render what assistance they could. The first who were found to have suffered, were a number of persons employed near the shaft – these miners having been burned when the flames from the furnace where driven along the workings. The volunteers' labours were arduous, for the explosion had so completely destroyed the ventilation that it was necessary to proceed with great caution and, of course, every delay only increased the fears for the safety of those walled in by the deadly choke-damp.

A few succeeded in penetrating the suffocating vapours and escaped with their lives, and one man who appeared dead, was brought back to life by the surgeon from Hindley, Mr Brayton, who applied artificial respiration for over ten minutes.

The rescuers were soon joined by miners from adjacent collieries all desperate to render what assistance they could. The catastrophe had been restricted to the west side seam and most of the victims appeared to have left their working places and were found in the main pony road, along which they had been trying to escape. Most of them looked as if placidly asleep, and only a few had been burned or bruised by the explosion.

The rescuers toiled until dusk by which time they had sent fifty seven bodies to the surface. The bodies as they were recovered, were taken to the workshop, in which a platform of loose boards had been hastily put together. The ill news had spread rapidly and a large crowd lined the path from the pit bank to the temporary mortuary.

The full extent of the disaster was apparent the following day when two more victims were discovered, and two of those rescued died from their injuries. The two bodies discovered were those of John Holcroft and Richard Beesley who had been struck by the full force of the blast, having been engaged 'holing' at the time of the explosion. Holcroft had been badly burned and Beesley had been buried beneath a fall of earth. In all, sixty one men had lost their lives and a number of others remained in the care of surgeon Brayton and his assistants.

The calamity was said to have rendered nearly fifty children fatherless and at several homes around the colliery, poverty stared the household in the face.

The case of the Tyldesley family was a very sorrowful one. The head of the family had died six weeks earlier, leaving eight children and a sickly wife. The bread winners of the household were four lads employed at the colliery, all of whom were at work on the ill fated morning. Of the four, two were dead and one was blinded by the disaster.

The Highton family also experienced the full horror of the situation. Firstly, the father was reported as safe and then the son was recovered from the pit, appearing to be none the worse for his ordeal. When the lad was returned home a clergyman accompanied him and a short prayer was offered for the mercy vouchsafe to the family. Alas, the joy was short lived because no sooner had the clergyman returned to the pit, than the body of the father was recovered and within another day the lad had gone into decline and died from his injuries.

Also amongst those killed was William Johnson, a miner who had been away from work ill for the previous nine weeks, and had only resumed his employment on the tragic morning. A widow and two children were left to mourn his departure.

Amongst those who escaped were a number of men at the far end of the workings, who at first tried to make their way to the pit shaft by the ordinary route. On their way, however, they came to a door and finding several bodies lying about they began to notice which way the current of air was blowing. Finding that the ventilation was completely reversed, they, after a short consultation, resolved to follow the wind, and so managed to reach the shaft.

A singular escape was made by a man named Ramsdale, who was working 400 or 500 yards from the pit eye. He knew exactly what had happened as soon as the sound of the explosion was heard in the workings. At once he threw down his tools and rushed along the level being soon met by the afterdamp. In his rush he came upon three young lads, who were screaming with terror, and had given themselves up for lost. Ramsdale told them to hold on by his trousers, and in that position he dragged them through the foul gas. After desperate efforts he reached the shaft with his charges all safe, and he sent the boys up first, feeling that he could stand the gas best.

The theory was that the explosion had been caused by "blowers", these being hollow places in the coal face containing gas. Often these were in such a state of compression that the gas rushed out like steam from a safety valve, filling miles of roadway and workings within a few seconds. All it would have taken to ignite the gas would have been the naked flame from a miners lamp.

A scientific writer in the 'Daily News' had been predicting colliery explosions for some days. He claimed that a sudden fall in the barometer readings had made the likelihood of a colliery explosion a distinct possibility. The management of the Hindley Green Colliery replied that there had been no fluctuation in their barometer readings and were adamant also that their tests regarding the amount of air passing through the mine had indicated no problems.

The inquest into the accident was opened at the Victoria Inn, close to the colliery, on the following Monday morning. Formal identification was provided for all the sixty one victims and permission was given to bury them.

That afternoon the scene at Hindley churchyard was one set to remain forever in the memory of those who witnessed it. The first hearse arrived at the church shortly before three o'clock, at which time the broad walk leading to the principal gate was lined on each side with spectators. It was bitterly cold. The approach of night was hastened by the dull foggy atmosphere and a fall of heavy rain, but the crowd kept its position and watched with deepest interest the arrival of each funeral cortege.

Hearse followed hearse in quick succession, and in a short time the ministers of the church proceeded to the gate and then all the bodies were borne in a long line to the church, followed by the troop of mourners. As the sacred edifice was entered the 'Dead March' was played upon the organ, and was continued whilst the coffins were placed along the north and south aisles. The service was conducted amidst the sorrowful scene and then the bodies were taken to their graves. As the mourners grouped themselves around the final resting places, the church bell continued to ring a mournful peel. By the time the clergymen had finished their sad office, darkness had fallen.

Postscript: The week had been a tragic one for Lancashire's workmen with five men being killed near Lancaster after an explosion at the Lowood Powder Works and two brothers being severely burned at the Pew Fall Colliery, Ashton-in-Makerfield, following a gas explosion.

Chapter 6

Murder of a Corporal

On Saturday the 20th of April 1833, three soldiers Corporal Daniel Maggs, Private William Hargreaves and Private John Roach, all members of the 85th Regiment of Foot, were assigned to the task of escorting a deserter from Manchester to Liverpool. That day they left the Infantry barracks in Regent Road, Salford and marched their prisoner from the New Bailey, Salford to Warrington.

The following morning they continued their trek to Liverpool and when they had gone a little along the way the deserter's wife, who was with them, asked the Corporal if her husband could have some breakfast. The party accordingly stopped at the nearest public house where Roach requested that the prisoner's handcuffs be removed while he ate his food. Corporal Maggs however was adamant that the deserter's hands should remain manacled and some angry words passed between him and Roach. The attitude of Private Roach was that his fellow soldiers were nothing more than cowards for sitting with their loaded muskets watching a man struggling to eat with handcuffs on. The Corporal's response was to warn Roach that if he did not watch what he said, he would be reported to the adjutant upon their return to the barracks. Roach responded by saying he did not care a damn, and when they were back on the road his threatening behaviour continued, including an utterance to the effect that he would shoot the Corporal with his loaded musket.

Once the deserter had been delivered, the men marched back to their barracks, and when they arrived on the Tuesday evening at nine o'clock, Corporal Maggs immediately arranged for John Roach to be detained in the guard-house, because of his behaviour on the road.

The following morning, despite being on a charge, Roach was permitted to leave the guard-house and take part in the routine parade. Once the parade was over, instead of returning to the guard-house, he marched straight to the barrack room in which Corporal Maggs lodged. The Corporal was in the company of a Private named Hugh Brown and was shocked to see Roach before him. Looking straight at the Corporal, Roach said, "Corporal Maggs, I am obliged to you for what you have done." To which the Corporal replied, "You know, John, it was your own fault". Without speaking another word Roach raised his musket and fired at the Corporal. The mouth of the piece was almost touching the Corporal when it was fired and he staggered and slumped to the floor. There was a fatal wound below his right breast and within five minutes he was dead.

After discharging his musket, Roach turned on his heels and reported back to the guard-house. It was there that a local police officer found Roach after being informed of the affair. When the officer quizzed him, Roach responded by saying that it had been the incident over the handcuffed deserter that had led to his action, telling the officer how they had marched for eight and twenty miles together on the return journey to their barracks without a word passing between them.

Within hours an inquest was held at the Duke of York, in Regent Road, Salford. On view was the body of Daniel Maggs, the deceased Irishman, who had been in the regiment for ten years and was highly respected by his comrades, as a quiet well-disposed man.

The trouble on the ill-fated escort duty was recounted and details of a row between the two fellow countrymen on St. Patrick's Day was revealed.

The bullet that mortally wounded Corporal Maggs was said to have been found at the foot of the stairs leading to the Corporal's room. After passing through the victim's body it was said to have gone through a lath and plaster partition, re-bounded against an opposite wall and fallen down the stairs.

The coroner listened to all the evidence and then remarked that it was perfectly clear and explicit and that he felt there were no extenuating circumstances. The jury agreed with the coroner's observations and John Roach was committed to Lancaster Castle for trial.

The trial of the 34-year-old Roach took place on Friday, August 16th 1833, in the Lancaster Assizes Crown Court. It took little time to present the prosecution case which included Private Hugh Brown's eye-witness account of the shooting.

When the prosecution evidence was complete His Lordship asked Roach if he had anything to say in his defence. The accused appeared much distressed and said, "I did it in a fatal moment, and without any intention to murder him. I was carried away in a moment of passion, and I am heartily sorry" – as he spoke his eyes filled with tears.

The only witness called by him was Captain William Hunter, an

On a Saturday in April, 1833, three soldiers called at the New Bailey Prison, Salford to collect a deserter.

officer of the regiment he had served for 15 years. He gave Roach an excellent character reference and stated that he believed him to be a religious man.

The learned Judge then summed up and the jury, after a moment's deliberation, found the prisoner guilty. Without putting on the black cap, His Lordship proceeded to pass sentence of death upon Roach.

At eight o'clock on the following Monday morning Roach, a native of Ireland and Roman Catholic, was brought out for execution. He walked with a quick and firm step, hardly glancing at the assembled crowd, and placed himself on the drop with his back to the people. Once the executioner had placed the cap over his head and adjusted the rope the Rev Brown, kneeling at the verge of the gallows, read the burial service. The service concluded the bolt was drawn and John Roach was launched into eternity. The platform however did not fall suddenly at once, but after descending a few inches remained stationary for a second or two before the final fall.

After hanging the usual time, the body was taken down and placed in a shell to be interred within the limits of the gaol. This was in accordance with the provisions of an Act of Parliament abolishing dissection as part of the punishment awarded against murderers.

Chapter 7

Motiveless Killing of a Wife

At about six o'clock on the evening of the 18th of April 1853, Richard Pedder, a man of about 50 years of age employed as a boatman on the Preston to Lancaster canal, entered the Shovels Inn at Hambleton, the village where he resided. Gaining the attention of the gathered assembly he coolly announced the death of his wife with the words, "I have killed our Bet".

Scarcely crediting the startling statement, two of the men present proceeded to Pedder's house for the purpose of satisfying themselves upon the matter. Once there, they discovered at the back of the premises, in the garden area, the lifeless body of Betty Pedder. The unfortunate woman was lying in a pool of blood, her head and face mutilated with gunshot wounds.

Within minutes Pedder returned to the house and proceeded to perform various strange vagaries. Firstly, he threw himself upon the ground by the side of the corpse, weeping and making other demonstrations of grief. He then appeared intent on taking his own life, initially with a shotgun that he set up in the garden, and then with a gun that he had loaded in the house. However the alertness of the men, by now gathered at the house, prevented such an occurrence by removing the guns from his possession.

In a wild and excitable mood Pedder then removed the body of his wife into the house where he laid it on the sofa. Shortly afterwards a police officer arrived and Pedder was conveyed to Stalmine police station. On the way there he stated that he had shot his wife from the kitchen window, adding, " I am a good shot; I aimed at the killing place, and that was her head". This statement he repeated several times but without assigning any reason for his terrible action.

In August of the same year Richard Pedder appeared at the Lancaster Summer Assizes charged with the wilful murder of Betty Pedder. The Defence Counsel attempted to convince the jury that the killing had been an accidental one. They argued that it was a moment of rashness and that the prisoner's conduct in giving himself up and with the emotion he displayed over the dead body, was inconsistent with the actions of a deliberate killer. They finally submitted to the

Richard Pedder entered the Shovels Inn at Hambleton and declared that he had killed his wife

jury that the death of the woman had been caused by an accidental shot and that the declaration alleged against him, "were wild and whirling words made when his reason reeled".

When the judge, Mr Justice Wightman summed up the trial proceedings, he pointed out that it was not until the coroners inquest that the suggestion of an accident was made. He observed that if it had been the case, then would not the prisoner have immediately proclaimed the manner in which his wife had met her death. Concerning the absence of a motive he stated that this was no reason to reduce the crime to manslaughter.

The jury deliberated for about ten minutes and then amidst a breathless silence delivered a verdict of "Wilful Murder", with a recommendation to mercy. His Lordship at once put on the black cap and addressed the prisoner in a most impressive tone and with marks of the deepest emotion. As the sentence of death was pronounced Richard Pedder, who had at times been much affected in the course of the trial, seemed almost unmoved. He was then led away without any outward signs of concern at his awful fate.

The jury's recommendation to mercy led to the drawing up of a petition to procure the reprieve of the condemned man. The vicar and the Mayor of Lancaster put their names at the head of the petition and in all some 530 signatures were gained.

The document set out the circumstances of the case and suggested that Pedder had committed the crime under the impulse of sudden passion or frenzy. The Home Secretary was unmoved by the plea and the Secretary of State replied that there were no grounds for interference with the course of justice. The execution was accordingly fixed to take place at noon, on the 27th of August and, with this in mind, executioner William Calcraft arrived the night before to prepare the scene.

There had been no executions in Lancaster for eighteen years and the event was anticipated with intense interest by those with a morbid taste for such painful exhibitions.

The early morning was gloomy and heavy rain fell at intervals, but this did not deter the tide of holiday-making people who rolled in from the surrounding districts. The crowd thronged the Castle parade and the adjacent churchyard which, from its elevation, commanded a complete view of the gallows and there, as a matter of course, front places were greatly in request. Most of the local factories ceased work at a half past eleven in order to give the work people an opportunity of witnessing the spectacle and of learning a moral lesson at the hands of the hangman.

When twelve o'clock arrived the church bell tolled the criminal's death knell and the door leading to the scaffold opened. Advancing with a firm and steady step Richard Pedder took his place under the fatal beam. As the executioner approached, Pedder inclined his head in order that Calcraft (who was not so tall as himself) might with greater facility adjust the noose and draw a white cap over his face. All was then still as the chaplain read the burial service and then the executioner completed his task with the drawing of the bolt. The drop fell, a few brief struggles on the part of the sufferer were perceptible and then all was over.

Pedder who was a powerfully built, broad chested man, about six feet tall, was executed in the attire worn during his trial, his clothes, similar to those usually seen on a labourer of the period, appeared to be rather tattered and old.

The crowd soon began to disperse and comparatively few remained until the expiration of an hour when the body was cut down to be interred within the precincts of the prison.

Chapter 8

Cold Blooded Mother's Crime

On the second Monday in March 1887, the newspapers of Lancashire announced to their readers that Elizabeth Berry, a former nurse at the Oldham Workhouse Infirmary, had that morning been executed at Walton Gaol. Three weeks earlier Mrs Berry, who was a widow, had been on trial at the Liverpool Assizes accused of the murder of her eleven-year-old daughter Edith.

For about five years the child had lived with her aunt, Ann Sanderson, at Miles Platting, her mother paying £12 a year towards her daughter's clothing and maintenance. The arrangement seemed to be a happy one with Mrs Berry paying visits whenever she could.

Over Christmas, 1886 mother and daughter were together at Miles Platting and when Mrs Berry had to return to her work at the Oldham Workhouse Infirmary her daughter pleaded to be able to join her there for a few days. It was eventually agreed that the child and a school friend would accompany Mrs Berry back to Oldham.

The children appeared to be having a good time when Mrs Sanderson received a letter through the post from young Edith. Alas, that communication was followed by a more dramatic one on the 3rd of January 1887, – it was a telegram which simply read, "COME AT ONCE, EDITH IS DYING!"

On the morning of New Years Day, Edith had been too ill to eat any breakfast and as the day progressed she had been vomiting. It was felt she had a stomach upset and the doctor prescribed a suitable medicine. Within forty eight hours the young girl had become inflicted with more pains and her pulse was barely noticeable. Amazed at the sudden decline of a healthy child the doctor became suspicious and came to the conclusion that she had possibly been poisoned. Although a mixture was prescribed and given to the girl, it was too late to save her, and early the next morning she died.

In view of these circumstances it was decided to carry out a post-mortem and three doctors who performed the examination came to the common conclusion; which was that as the body showed no signs of natural disease, and as her stomach and intestines had marks

The Oldham Workhouse Infirmary where young Edith was poisoned in January 1887

of blood upon them, and her throat appeared black and corroded, she had died due to the intake of a corrosive poison. The poison probably disappearing during her bouts of vomiting, consequently leaving no trace in the body.

Almost at once suspicion began to fall on to Mrs Berry, who had access to the Infirmary dispensary, where a supply of sulphuric acid was kept. Although a death certificate was obtained, stating that cause of death was acute inflammation of the stomach and bowels, the rumours abounded.

Suspicions were enough to satisfy an inquest jury, who gave a verdict of wilful murder against Mrs Berry – and it was on the coroner's warrant that she was sent for trial at Liverpool Assizes. In the meantime the Oldham Magistrates had concluded their hearing by stating that due to a lack of motive Mrs Berry had no case to answer.

The trial took place before Mr Justice Hawkins and the prosecution claimed that the prisoner had poisoned the girl in order to obtain £10 on a life insurance policy, and to rid herself of the £12 per year upkeep costs.

In response, the defending Counsel suggested that the mother was kind and affectionate and claimed the suggestion that she would kill her own child for money was a monstrous proposition. His Lordship, during his summing up, pointed out that the woman had made several false statements relative to the child's health and the insurance upon her. The jury took little time to reach a verdict and within ten minutes Mrs Berry was being sentenced to death for what Mr Justice Hawkins described as a cold blooded, merciless and cruel murder.

Unbeknown to that jury, the suspicions surrounding the daughter's death had led the police to investigate the death of Mrs Berry's mother in February 1886. Mrs Finley, like her granddaughter, had died suddenly and the Home Secretary granted permission for the body to be exhumed. Once again the examination did not rule out poisoning and the symptoms of the two deaths were alarmingly similar.

Elizabeth Berry had also, on that occasion, profited from an insurance pay-out and suspicion was enough for another coroner's warrant to be issued with a verdict of wilful murder against her.

By this time Mrs Berry was already awaiting sentence of death so the case was not proceeded any further.

Not unnaturally, rumours also circulated with regard to the deaths of her husband Thomas, and their son, Harold. The father had died in the summer of 1881 after being ill for sometime and young Harold had, in the autumn of 1882, become ill and died after a trip to the seaside. On both occasions Elizabeth Berry was said to have benefited from insurance policy payments. However, these accusations, like

Elizabeth Berry, a former nurse, was sentenced to hang

the one concerning her mother, were to lay unproven as the former nurse awaited her fate.

On the Saturday before her execution, Mrs Berry was visited by her solicitor who was intending to make arrangements for the woman's worldly affairs. On entering the prison he was taken to interview her from the opposite side of a steel mesh partition. She was dressed in prison garb, and wore a blue serge dress, white collar, and white cap. As soon as she saw the solicitor, who had been very kind to her during her imprisonment, she fell into a swoon. Two doctors were promptly in attendance and it was three or four hours before she recovered. Later in the day the solicitor was once again admitted and was able to attend to the matters in hand.

From the time of receiving her sentence the 31-year-old Elizabeth Berry had gradually declined and had expressed a desire not to see any visitors. Preferring to spend her remaining hours in solitude, she was in a penitent mood, passing her time in devotional exercises.

Early on the morning of the execution, a heavy hailstorm passed over Liverpool accompanied by a peal of thunder and a flash of lightening. This was followed by a fall of a snow which ceased shortly before the hour fixed for Mrs Berry's execution. The snow lay thickly on the ground and the air was bitingly keen.

Outside Walton Gaol a very small crowd had collected, consisting mainly of men on their way to work. There were a few women mixed with the crowd and they were generally sympathetic; hoping that the culprit would be reprieved. The tolling of the prison bell, however, dispelled those hopes and the crowd kept at a distance from the gaol by a police cordon, waited patiently for the hoisting of the black flag.

Meanwhile James Berry, the executioner, was busy inside the gaol, hastening the preparations for the final scene. An hour earlier the chaplain had visited the condemned woman in her cell. She had passed a very restless night, and rose un-refreshed and nervous. After receiving the spiritual consolation of the chaplain, she made a statement to him persisting in her innocence of the crime for which she was about to suffer.

Berry had remained in the gaol all night and along with the prisoner and gaol officials he proceeded to the scaffold. The condemned woman, who wore a black silk dress, was supported by two warders and she repeated earnestly and distinctly the responses to the chaplain's exhortations. Once Berry had completed his preparations, the bolt was drawn and the drop fell, the woman dying without the faintest struggle. At eight o'clock that morning, Mrs Berry had become the first person to be executed at Walton Gaol.

Postscript: Years later James Berry, when recalling the execution of Mrs Berry, revealed that he had, in his younger days, danced with her at a police ball in Manchester. On the night before the execution he had sat with her and reassured her that he would not keep her alive a moment longer than necessary. After he had completed the task the former Bradford policeman took a lock of her hair to add to his souvenirs.

Chapter 9

The Killing of Sergeant Brett

In the middle of the nineteenth century the Irish were a famished people who, hit by the potato blight, found themselves in great distress. They had no money for even the cheapest food and as they starved economic necessity saw boats loaded with cattle, butter and cheese leave the Irish ports. Their government were urged to close the ports and distribute the food in their own country, but they were reluctant to do so for fear of interfering with their trade agreements.

As a consequence it was reckoned that over a million people in Ireland died of starvation and disease, a quarter of a million managed to get to England and a further million embarked for America in crowded and insanitary ships. The exiles carried with them bitter memories and nursed a hatred against England which had let them starve, while boats left their country laden with food produced in Ireland.

The Irish in America never forgot the land of their origin and they formed a society called the 'Irish Republican Brotherhood' or 'Fenians' as it was commonly known. They collected money to send to Ireland and the cash was used to purchase arms for the branches formed on both sides of the Atlantic.

By 1867 the Fenian movement was a substantial organisation and, according to informers, plans were afoot to stage an uprising on the English mainland. Acting on the intelligence received, the authorities were alert enough to seek out the leaders before any outbreak of anarchy could occur.

To this end on the 11th of September 1867, four suspicious looking fellows were observed by the police, loitering about the streets of Shude-hill, in Manchester. They were closely watched, and in the course of time they divided into couples. Two of the four men were seen to enter a house under circumstances which still further strengthened the suspicions of the police.

Assistance was secured, and the two men were taken into custody, not, however without a severe struggle. Fortunately for them the

The killing of Sergeant Brett, a father of ten, was regarded as an outrage

officers discovered the men they were wrestling with were armed with revolvers and only prompt action enabled them to be disarmed.

The two men thus apprehended gave their names as John Wright and Martin Williams. Communication followed with the constabulary of Ireland, London and Liverpool and as a result little time was lost in identifying the two prisoners as the notorious and somewhat celebrated Fenian Head Centres, Colonel Kelly and Captain Deasey, both of whom were 'wanted' in Ireland. They being the right-hand and most trusted lieutenants of the head of all Head Centres, James Stephens, who placed the most implicit confidence in the judgement and ability of the pair.

In the regions of Swansea Street, Carter Street and Rochdale Road, Stephens was the one who was to 'ride the cowardly Saxons to the ground'. Many a night when a 'drop of the crater' had loosened the tongues, the Irish denizens of Angels Meadow delighted themselves and their companions by singing songs of the most Fenian type in the public bars and beer houses.

Convinced that they had captured the real and true Kelly and Deasey, of Fenian celebrity, the authorities produced the necessary warrants for their remand. It was subsequently arranged for the pair to be taken before the Magistrates at the city police court in Manchester. This necessitated the removal of the prisoners from the city gaol and their transportation to the opposite side of Manchester in a prison van.

The hearing was a brief one and the remand insisted on by a member of the Metropolitan force was as a matter of course endorsed. The whole episode had caused great excitement in Manchester and as the police prepared to return the two prisoners to the Belle Vue prison, many people gathered to witness the departure of the prison van.

Both Kelly and Deasey were handcuffed and placed in separate compartments at the end of the van nearest the driver, they, along with some thirty-seven other prisoners being confined for the return journey to the City Gaol. Six policemen and the driver sat outside the van and a seventh officer, Sergeant Charles Brett, a man highly respected in the police force, took his position inside the vehicle. Behind was a cab containing four other constables, all, like officers on the prison van, being unarmed.

The crowd that witnessed the departure was considerably larger than ordinarily and amongst them were several strangers who mingled freely with the throng, tuning very impudently sundry Fenian verses.

Nothing to create suspicion was observed as the van proceeded through the city; but as soon as it had passed through the railway arch on the Hyde Road, a man ran into the middle of the carriageway and discharged a revolver at the horses. The shots took effect on the animals, one of them being seriously injured, and the other wounded in the neck. The result being that one of the horses reared and plunged and the van was brought to a sudden halt.

Several shots were then fired from a mob which the abutments of the railway arch had concealed from the approaching vehicle. The mob, consisted of some forty persons with at least fifteen in possession of revolvers, with a couple more brandishing single-barrelled pistols. Shot followed upon shot in quick succession, and bricks and other missiles were freely hurled at the police. The determined

As the prison van passed through the railway arch, the attackers were waiting.

ruffians then firing at the officers on the roof of the van, who, together with those in the cab found it necessary to retire some distance down the road.

The mob then tried with the aid of large stones to break in the roof and door of the vehicle, and also endeavoured to force open the latter by shooting into the keyhole of the lock. At length they effected an entry, and one of them demanded the keys from Sergeant Brett.

He refused to deliver them up and was immediately shot in the head, a ball entering his forehead on the right side and passing out at the back of his head. The assailants then freed Kelly and Deasey and, seizing the opportunity, four female prisoners also escaped.

While this outrage was in perpetration the police officers several times attempted to charge upon the mob, but as they were unarmed, save for a few sticks and a truncheon or two, and as their assailants met every approach with a discharge of revolvers, their attempts were fruitless. Many civilians took part with the police, but without arms resistance was useless. Some idea of the fray being formed by the fact that in all upwards of one hundred shots were fired.

Information of the attack was speedily conveyed to Fairfield Street Station and at once a body of constables armed with cutlasses was dispatched. By the time they reached the scene of the outrage the Fenians had withdrawn, running as a body over the fields to the north of Hyde Road and across the railway embankment.

A pursuit was at once started and a man named Michael Larkin, from Eliza Street in the city, was soon captured having tripped while crossing the railway. He was believed to have been the man who fired upon the horses and in his possession was a revolver. Another young man, named William O'Mara Allen of Suddell Street on the Oldham Road was keenly pursued. Said to have been the one who gunned Sergeant Brett down he was chased across the fields and the railway and whenever anyone got near him he pointed his pistol in their direction. He maintained the flight until he was overpowered by some civilians in a brickcroft near to the Ashton New Road. Being knocked down and treated with considerable violence, he was only given up alive following the intercession of the police.

As the evening advanced the police scoured the quarters of the town most frequented by the supporters of the Fenian movement, and before midnight some twenty persons were in custody.

Sergeant Brett had been removed to the Royal Infirmary, where, at half past five o'clock he died from the wound inflicted on him.

Many of the police officers had narrowly escaped injury while two of them needed urgent medical attention, one following a shot through the left thigh and another after receiving a shot in his right foot.

The outrage of the 18th of September had caused considerable feeling against the Fenians, particularly the killing of Sergeant Brett, an old and respected officer who left a wife and ten children most who fortunately, were grown up. Ironically, had he survived a few more trips on the prison van he would have been eligible to be pensioned off.

Various arrests and trials took place in October and November and sentences of varying degrees were pronounced. The special commission who presided over the investigation ordered the execution of five men, William O'Mara Allen, Michael Larkin, William Gould, Edward Shore and Michael Maguire. However, before the execution date was set Maguire, a 32-year-old clothes dealer, was given an unconditional pardon while Edward Shore, a 26-year-old traveller, received a respite of his sentence.

It was then announced that the executions would take place at the New Bailey, Salford, on Saturday the 23rd of November 1867. At once active measures were taken to overawe any attempt at a rescue or breach of the peace. The Home Secretary deemed that it was the duty of the civil authorities to prepare a civil force to carry out the due administration of the law. To this end a large number of special constables were recruited and for three days prior to the execution date, the Mayor was busily engaged in swearing in over two thousand volunteers.

Barriers were erected along the main thoroughfare leading to the New Bailey and the Mayors of Manchester, Salford, Bolton and other adjoining districts requested the well-disposed portion of the inhabitants to keep away from the execution.

Although the civil authorities took on themselves the responsibility for law and order, arrangements were made to have military aid stationed in the vicinity if the situation became difficult.

During the Friday, particularly towards evening, the streets in the vicinity of the New Bailey were crowded with spectators, anxious to get a glimpse of the scaffold. Detectives were also to be seen quietly and unobtrusively watching the departure and arrival of persons. In the evening, the masons and carpenters were engaged in completing the scaffold and the large gathering took a great interest in the proceedings.

There was no apparent gathering of suspicious groups at street corners, or anything to indicate that the 'brotherhood', to which the convicts were said to belong, would attempt any violence, or interfere in any way with the course of the law. The general feeling was that the sentence was deserved; although sorrow was expressed on account of the youth of Allen, and because of the wife and family of Larkin.

In the darkness and gloom of the night the scaffold looked a most sombre object, and stood out in bold and startling relief. The night was clear and starlight; but as the morning wore on heavy mist prevailed.

The culprits had retired to bed at half past eleven. They seemed to rest quietly, and at the time appointed for rising on the Saturday morning – shortly before five o'clock- they were asleep. They were directly woken and, after dressing, were attended by three local clergymen who said Mass in their Roman Catholic faith.

At a quarter past seven the three men partook of breakfast, the allowance being a pint of coffee and a round of toast. After breakfast and up to the time of pinioning, the culprits were earnestly engaged in religious exercise with the attendant priests.

As the time fast approached eight o'clock the waiting crowd, which numbered some fifteen thousand, looked anxiously towards the door at the rear of the scaffold through which the condemned men would enter into their gaze.

At three minutes past the appointed hour the door opened and the fatal procession appeared. There was a cry of "hats off" and the great bulk in the street near the scaffold seemed to obey the order. Allen was the first of the culprits to make an appearance and he was accompanied by a clergyman who was reading the Miserere. He had a very haggard look considering his youth and obviously felt the situation he was in.

Calcraft, the executioner, followed him on to the scaffold, accompanied by an assistant and in no time had selected Allen's position on the drop and placed the white cap over his victim's head and face.

Next to appear was Gould, who went directly toward Allen, grabbing hold of his hands and kissing him. The stoutest of the three men Gould had a somewhat quiet and easy appearance. Calcraft quickly positioned the second man and then turned his attention to the final convict, Larkin. After the white cap had been drawn over his head and the rope adjusted he seemed to lean to one side, as if in a fainting condition.

Calcraft wasted no time, the bolt was drawn and the three men fell out of sight of the watching crowd, their hanging bodies being hidden behind the black cloth that draped the scaffold. Allen appeared to die instantaneously, Gould seemed to swing about for a few seconds and Larkin struggled for about two minutes, until his lifeless body brought the punishment of the law to its conclusion.

The bodies, each of which had a cross hanging on their breast, were left suspended for an hour before Calcraft completed his appointed task by cutting them down and delivering them to within the precincts of the gaol.

Postscript: Allen was said to have been engaged to a cousin and within days the following verse was published, dedicated to his sweetheart. They were claimed to be the last written words of the condemned man.

TO MISS MARY —— ——.

Oh, my love, I am parting from you; pray that we meet in Heaven. May God, in His mercy, protect you. I cannot write much to-day, Mary dear. We must think of the other world.

May heaven be your bed, Mary,
May the Holy Cross be your guide;
Oh, remember your dear William,
And don't throw him aside.

Oh, Mary dear, we have to part,
No more I'll walk on Erin's shore;
Still let me rest in your fond heart,
For now and evermore.

I did not see you, Mary,
Since I was condemned to die;
Oh! you'll not forget me, Mary,
But for me you will not sigh.

Oh! Mary, if I had your heart,
I would clasp it to my breast,
And from me it would not part
Until I was laid to rest.

When I am dead and gone,
Think that I am all alone;
Remember, still, my heart was won
By you, when we were far from home.

Good bye for evermore, and may God protect you. These are the dying wishes of your true lover, W. P. ALLEN.

From the *Preston Guardian* newspaper

Chapter 10

A Deathly Drunken Brawl

On a Saturday afternoon in March 1898, two men while under the influence of alcohol, commenced to quarrel outside the New Inn public house at the corner of Barkerhouse Road and Leeds Road in Nelson. The participants were Robert Thistlethwaite, aged 21, a weaver of Barrowford and Joseph Houldsworth, aged 24, a carter from Elm Street, Nelson.

The pair soon got to blows with Houldsworth seeming to be having the better of the exchanges. For a couple of minutes they rolled around the ground intent of doing mischief to each other. Then Thistlethwaite appeared to slink away and went into a nearby alley-way. Within a minute however, he had re-emerged and without speaking suddenly dealt Houldsworth a blow with his fist, in which was concealed a pocket knife with its open blade.

As Thistlethwaite turned to walk away Houldsworth screamed out, "Oh, he's stabbed me" and a number of onlookers went to the injured man's assistance. A local doctor who witnessed the incident immediately came to Houldsworth's aid and laid him on his back. Despite his expert knowledge he could do little for the man and within a minute Houldsworth was dead.

Local constables were alerted to the incident and Thistlethwaite was at once detained by the officers. In his pocket was the blood-stained knife he had used and he appeared far from sober when arrested. As Thistlethwaite was escorted to the police station a large crowd followed behind. He seemed unconscious of what had occurred and once in the station he sat with his head buried in his hands. The police decided that it would be best to wait until he had recovered from his bacchanalian stupor before making the formal charge of causing Houldsworth's death.

The crowd outside the police station soon had something else to attract their attention and this was the carrying though the streets of the dead body on a stretcher. The victims clothing was terribly stained with blood due to the fact that the main artery in his neck had been completely severed. Houldsworth had been a fine strapping fellow with an excellent character. Originally he came from Silsden in Yorkshire and was married with three children.

The general opinion was that he had been averse to fighting Thistlethwaite and it was only great provocation that made him want to settle the matter. Thistlethwaite on the other hand was described in less complimentary terms by his associates. Amongst his mates he was described as a regular "Do nowt", and it was said he had contemplated violence on other occasions. A native of Colne he had at the time of the incident been married for 18 months, being the father of one child, which was unfortunately blind. His marriage had been far from harmonious and in fact, he had been convicted on one occasion for assaulting his wife. It also transpired that he had in the past remarked to this mates that he would "end his days on the scaffold" and that he would "never die a natural death".

These words must have been on his mind on Thursday, April 21st, 1898 when he appeared at Manchester Assizes before Mr Justice Ingham charged with the Wilful Murder of Joseph Houldsworth. Thistlethwaite pleaded not guilty to the charge and was accommodated with a chair as the proceedings got underway. Long discussions and varying evidence, as to the nature of the fight followed, and a witness stated that Houldsworth, who had apparently won the exchanges, remarked, "I'll let thee alone, I'll let thee get up". The prosecution outlined the circumstances that led to the fight and according to witnesses Houldsworth had approached the prisoner and made some remark about an assault that the prisoner had apparently committed on a friend of the deceased a short time before. The prisoner was then said to have remarked that he "would do the same to him" and then a kind of challenge took place.

The defence Counsel reminded the jury that it is not every killing that is murder by a long way, and that before the prisoner can be convicted of murder they must be satisfied that he inflicted the wound maliciously. While not using drink as an excuse for the crime, he claimed that because of the man's condition through drink that no intent could be possible.

At this point the Judge asked the prosecution if, on the evidence presented, they wished to press the capital charge stating that in his opinion he did not think it was a case of murder. The prosecution then indicated their willingness to accept a lesser charge and the defence agreed that manslaughter would be more appropriate.

The defence Counsel then continued with his address to the jury and told them that the prisoner being a smaller man than his victim, really thought he was in peril and it was under those circumstances he used the knife. He remarked that Thistlethwaite did not deny causing the man's death, but that the circumstances indicated manslaughter a more appropriate verdict.

The jury thereupon found the prisoner not guilty of murder and Thistlethwaite was then formally charged with manslaughter. The jury were again asked for their verdict and he was convicted of the lesser offence. Asked if he had anything to say he replied, "I am guilty of manslaughter".

His Lordship, addressing Thistlethwaite, pointed out that this crime like so many others was due to drink. He then discussed the use of the knife and the assumption that he may have used it in his own defence, fearing he was in danger. However he stated that he must make an example of him as a warning to others in a similar position. It should be a warning to others to avoid drink and to hesitate before pulling out deadly weapons. He then sentenced the prisoner to five years penal servitude.

On receiving his sentence the prisoner seemed somewhat surprised and relieved at his Lordship's leniency.

Chapter 11

A Hotel Cook's Terrible End

On Sunday October the 13th, 1895 the staff and residents of the Foxhall Hotel, Blackpool were stunned by the dreadful tragedy that had occurred within their midst.

Just prior to tea time the head waiter, to his surprise, noticed that the cook, Mrs Sarah Toomey, had not laid the cloth for tea as was her duty. He went upstairs and knocked on her room door to enquire if she intended going downstairs. Receiving no answer he entered the room and was horrified to find the cook on the floor, with her throat cut from ear to ear. Under her body was found a knife.

An investigation got underway immediately and enquiries were made as to the whereabouts of the unfortunate woman's husband. At once a search began for John Toomey who had also been employed at the hotel as a kitchen porter. The couple resided at the popular establishment and they had retired together to Mrs Toomey's room, shortly after lunch time.

It was concluded that any struggle that occurred must have been very slight and no one on the premises could recall hearing anything unusual. Immediate impressions were of suicide but this was soon dispelled by the finding of a clasp knife and the apparent flight of the dead woman's husband.

The origin of the knife was soon discovered and an ironmonger from South Shore informed the police of Toomey's purchase of the weapon on the Friday before the incident. As additional facts came to light there seemed not the least doubt that the crime was premeditated and drink and jealousy seemed to be the prime motives.

The couple's grown up children told how John Toomey had on numerous occasions threatened the well being of his wife and that their marriage had been a catalogue of threats. Daughters and son alike told of the unwarranted suspicions of John Toomey, who often accused his wife of unfaithful carrying-ons. In recent weeks he had suggested that she was being too familiar with waiters at the Blackpool hotel.

When the inquest on the death of Sarah Toomey was held the

Inside the Foxhall Hotel, Sarah Toomey was discovered with her throat cut

following Tuesday, the witnesses confirmed the evidence that had appeared in the local papers. A threatened wife and a jealous husband were said to be the ingredients for the tragic occurrence.

One of the witnesses called was William Green Brookes, a cellar man from the Palatine Hotel, Blackpool, who stated that he knew the missing husband by sight and had been in the Red Lion, Bispham along with him at half past four on the afternoon of the killing. On entering the bar parlour he had seen Toomey who was sat reading a newspaper and having a drink and a cigar. Toomey, who appeared quite sober, asked Brookes to have a drink with him, which he did.

He then asked him if he could do a favour for him and take a note to a Mrs Morris, the daughter of Toomey, along with £2.14s.0d, a watch and a chain. Toomey explained that he was going away to Belfast and his daughter needed the money to pay her rent. The witness agreed to the request and noticing that Toomey seemed to be very much down told him to keep his "pecker up".

During the inquest the note was read out and simply said, "Half this is for Lucy and half for May". According to the witness, Toomey remained in the bar a further 20 minutes and then left, walking off in the direction of Fleetwood.

Towards the end of the inquest there was a dramatic turn of events

John Toomey visited the Red Lion at Bispham and asked a favour

when it was revealed that clothing belonging to Toomey had been found by the seashore. A waistcoat was produced and Toomey's daughter identified it as part of her father's clothing. The indication was that he had committed suicide and the coroner ordered the inquest to be adjourned until a later date.

Two weeks later the mystery was complete when a dock labourer from Fleetwood picked up the body on the shore at high tide. He and others had watched it float in on the Monday morning tide.

Once again on Tuesday, October the 26th, the tragedy occupied the thoughts of the Blackpool public when the inquest into the affair continued. The decomposed body of Toomey was identified by both a daughter and son of the 56-year-old kitchen porter.

His son told the inquest that in his opinion his father was not in his right mind. He recalled how on the Thursday before his mother's death, the father had been on bad terms with his wife and had shown it in his looks. He had showed signs of temper for a number of years but it had grown noticeably worse in the recent past.

The coroner, in the course of his summing up, briefly traced the movements of the murderer and described the callous indifference he had shown at the Red Lion, Bispham shortly after his terrible deed. The question, he reminded the jury, was the state of the man's mind at the time he took his life. He referred to the son and daughter's remarks that their father was queer in his head and stated that there was little foundation for such claims.

The coroner said that, in his opinion, the evidence if well and carefully considered, implied that Toomey was perfectly sane at the time of his actions. He pointed out that Toomey had in fact shaved his moustache off, evidently with the intention of eluding the police, but altering his mind he had fallen back upon his original plan of throwing himself into the ocean.

The jury, without hesitation, immediately recorded a verdict of "felo-de-se" on the Foxhall Hotel killer.

At the conclusion of the inquiry the coroner handed the burial certificate to Toomey's son who afterwards took charge of the body and conveyed it to Blackpool for burial.

Chapter 12

Not A Murderer in Sight

Once again in March 1813, twenty of the County's most respected gentlemen gathered in Lancaster to serve as Grand Jurors at the forthcoming Assizes. Ahead of them was a fortnight of intense deliberations that would determine the fate of the latest collection of alleged 19th century wrongdoers.

Burglary, highway robbery, pocket picking, horse stealing, murder and the uttering of forged notes were amongst the crimes set to be brought before Mr Baron Thomson. The previous Assizes had ended with five men being executed for forgery, highway robbery, burglary and wounding. Consequently there was much public interest in the proceedings and great anxiety amongst those who stood on trial for their very lives.

The second day of the proceedings aroused much interest with the appearance in court of two women charged with forging and uttering counterfeit bank notes, knowing them to be forged.

First to face the glare of the packed court-room was Elizabeth Dewhurst who, the prosecution claimed, was a very considerable dealer in forged notes. Because of this they stated she had been marked out for detection by the agents of the Bank of England.

The court heard that a preconcerted scheme was devised in a bid to ensnare her. A witness by the name of James Platt told the court that on the 16th of October last, he had gone to the Manchester home of the accused at around three o'clock in the afternoon. Invited inside by her he asked if she had got 'anythings' (which was the term made use of to signify bank notes), to which she replied that she had. Platt requested that she bring the 'things' to his master's warehouse in Market Street Lane, Manchester. She agreed to do so, but said it would be after five o'clock as she could not leave home immediately. Before he left she explained to him that she had none but the 'old sort', which he understood meant two pound notes.

Platt then told the court how he made arrangements with a police officer named Joseph Nadin to set the final trap for the accused. The officer concealed himself in the warehouse in a position to enable him to witness the transaction between Platt and the woman.

Some half an hour later than expected Elizabeth Dewhurst arrived at the warehouse and, according to Platt, in her hand was a parcel containing the forged notes. Then in view of the watching officer, Platt took out of his pocket six good one pound notes and in return received five forged two pound notes. Elizabeth Dewhurst then left the warehouse unaware of the fact that she had been observed carrying out the transaction.

Officer Nadin completely corroborated the evidence of Platt and an inspector of notes from the Bank of England confirmed that the ones received from Elizabeth Dewhurst were forgeries.

The defence set up on the part of the prisoner was that she went with the parcel to the warehouse at the request of her husband and without any knowledge of the contents. A witness on her behalf, Sarah Wright, claimed that she had been with her when she was given the parcel by her husband who had instructed her to go to the warehouse in Market Street Lane. She described the parcel as being wrapped in brown paper and tied with a string. Officer Nadin was called again and he stated that the parcel containing the notes was not wrapped in brown paper but in a leaf torn out of a book.

Police Officer Joseph Nadin was called to give evidence

Elizabeth Dewhurst had, the court was told, been apprehended in January in Leeds, but the six pounds paid to her were not then in her possession.

The jury, after their deliberations, returned a verdict of guilty on the counts of the indictment and she was returned to the cells to await her sentence.

Later on the same day Martha Hughes appeared before the Grand Jury charged with a similar set of offences. Once again James Platt and Officer Nadin were the main witnesses for the prosecution.

Platt told the court that he had known the prisoner very well, and knew her to be a dealer in bad notes. It was therefore agreed between himself and Officer Nadin that he should go to the shop of the prisoner and purchase from her some notes, whilst Nadin remained on the outside of the shop door and observed what passed within.

Platt accordingly entered the shop of the prisoner and enquired of her if she had 'anythings' to which request she beckoned him to enter the back room, which he did. She then asked him how many he wanted to which he answered, "Three two's". At first the woman said he should only have one, "No", said Platt, "I wish to have three".

Upon his insistence the prisoner gave Platt three two pound forged bank notes and in return he gave the woman four good one pound notes. After the bargain was completed, and whilst the transaction was going on, the husband of Martha Hughes looked into the room and said, "get on".

Relative to this point an objection was raised by the prisoner's Counsel that the wife was under the cohesion of her husband. To this end they cited several cases to prove that under such circumstances Martha Hughes should be acquitted.

Baron Thomson said he recognised the Rule of Law stressed by the prisoner's Counsel, but thought the case did not come within that Rule, saying he was of the opinion that the crime, in this case, was complete before the husband appeared.

When Joseph Nadin was called he corroborated the testimony of Platt and an examiner of the Bank of England proved the forgery. Several witnesses were called on the part of the prisoner, but the jury had little hesitation in bringing in a verdict of Guilty.

On Saturday, April 3rd, 1813 as the Assizes drew to a close, Baron Thomson addressed a gathering of seventeen convicted persons in the following manner – "You unhappy prisoners now before me have been severally convicted of various offences against the laws of your country, for which by those laws your lives are justly forfeited". In particular he addressed his remarks to five men, Thomas Dwyer, Tobias Toole, John Davies, Timothy O'Brien and James Rogers. He told them that they were part of a formidable band which for some considerable time had annoyed the neighbourhood of Liverpool, by attacking and raiding His Majesty's subjects on the highway. The crime that Dwyer, Toole and Davies were convicted on, involved attacking a coach in the night, firing a pistol into the coach filled with six persons, and committing robbery. Unfortunately for the prisoners, among the occupants of the coach were men who had gone out for the purpose of apprehending and convicting the persons engaged in these frequent robberies.

O'Brien and Rogers were convicted of a robbery at a different time but although their crime did not have the same outrage and violence as the former one, His Lordship felt it merited a severe and necessary punishment.

Turning his attention to the matter of criminals found guilty of disposing of forged notes, purporting them to be notes of the Bank of England, he first addressed a prisoner by the name of Robert Barber. He reminded him that he had been convicted on two accounts of passing five pound notes and that he had made a vain and idle attempt of accounting for how the notes arrived in his possession. In His Lordships opinion, there was no doubt of his guilt and the prisoner was told to prepare himself for the awful consequence of his conviction.

He then addressed Martha Hughes and Elizabeth Dewhurst and reminded them that they stood before him guilty of similar offences to those committed by Robert Barber. To them however, he gave a glimmer of hope, telling them that a review of their cases would take place, and that if any circumstances appeared to make them the objects of Royal Mercy, they should be eternally grateful.

The outcome of the later deliberations was that the two women were ordered to be transported for the remainder of their lives.

Three weeks later on Saturday, April 24th six men, Dwyer, Davies, O'Brien, Toole and Rogers convicted of highway robbery, and Barber guilty of uttering forged notes, were led onto the scaffold at Lancaster Castle. All attempts to save the lives of the offenders had failed and they were handed over to resident executioner Edward Barlow, who despatched them from this life.

On October the 2nd of the same year two more men, James Thorpe (alias Allen) and Robert Dewhurst were publicly executed under the walls of Lancaster Castle. Thorpe was convicted on a charge of highway robbery and Dewhurst for uttering forged bank notes.

Dewhurst was in fact the husband of Elizabeth Dewhurst who had been convicted at the previous Assizes. Unlike his wife, Robert Dewhurst received no reprieve from his sentence being regarded as a notorious dealer in forged notes.

With not a murderer in sight so ended the executions for 1813 – eight in all. Once again the Grand Jurors had performed their tasks and the Justices had imposed the sentences necessary, in their view, to maintain law and order. Both highway robbery and forgery were prevalent at the time and they had issued the ultimate deterrent.

Lancaster Castle's resident hangman, Edward 'Ned' Barlow awaited the next collection of villains

Chapter 13

Robbery on The Highway

On the last Friday in April 1818, a gentleman was returning to his home in Edge Hill, Liverpool when he was stopped near the Botanic Gardens by two footpads. One of them held a pistol to his head while the other took from him his watch and several papers.

The following morning before nine o'clock two men appeared at a pawn brokers in Liverpool's Tythebarn Street and pawned the stolen watch.

On the evening of the same day Robert Pendleton, a farmer of West Derby near Liverpool, was returning from a trip to the city when he was approached by two men who asked him for directions. The meeting was in Breck Lane, Everton and after he had pointed the way, one of the men grabbed him by the coat and asked him if he had any money. "Some little, not much" was the reply. At this they produced a pistol which one of them pointed at his head while the other relieved him of his watch, 2s.6d. in silver and a double clasp penknife which he had in his pocket.

Warning Pendleton not to speak a word they then hurried off in the direction of Liverpool. Once the robbers were out of sight, Pendleton vaulted a wall and ran through the fields to get ahead of them, returning to the road some distance in front of his attackers. Almost immediately an acquaintance of his, William Kelly, appeared on the scene and as Pendleton related his distressing experience they heard the tread of persons approaching.

As they came in to view Pendleton recognised them as his assailants and exclaimed, "Here they are Kelly, thee fasten on one, I'll fasten on the other". The pair instantly sprang at the ruffians and a desperate struggle ensued, during which the villains drew out shoemakers knifes. Both Kelly and Pendleton courageously held on to the men despite receiving cuts and stab wounds. Fortunately the road was a much frequented one and soon a number of men were on hand to aid the two heroes. As they approached they heard Kelly saying, "Damn, thee villain, I have fastened on thee now, and while I have breath in my body, I'll not quit thee".

Once the two men were properly secured, Pendleton turned to them and said "Damn thee, thee little know Bob Pendleton, if thee thought to rob him and get off without a tussle for it!". The two robbers were then taken to the Everton Watch-house, where the stolen property was found upon their persons. Also in their possession were items which, in value and description, matched those taken from a man and a woman on the Derby Road less than an hour earlier.

Both Pendleton and Kelly, married men with large families, received a number of wounds at the hands of their assailants and Kelly, the most severely wounded, was conveyed to the Infirmary.

The two robbers were identified as Daniel and William Fitzpatrick and immediately they were suspected of being responsible for many robberies committed in the neighbourhood during the previous winter. The men were cousins and a search of their Liverpool dwelling house on the following Sunday led to the discovery of articles taken in the Friday evening attack near the Botanic Gardens.

Described as ill-looking desperate men the Fitzpatricks were examined in the Town Hall and following the evidence of various witnesses they were committed to Lancaster Castle for trial at the next Assizes.

The Lancaster Assizes were held in August 1818, and the Fitzpatricks were among the 46 prisoners who appeared before the Hon. Baron Wood and the Hon. Mr Justice Bayley. To the charge of highway robbery at Everton and Liverpool, both 25-year-old William Fitzpatrick and 22-year-old Daniel Fitzpatrick pleaded guilty, saying they had neither counsel, money, nor friends, and that it was of no use to deny.

His Lordship, however, urged them to plead not guilty and assured them that any Gentleman of the Bar would willingly conduct their defence. The cousins replying, "Well, we don't care – Not Guilty".

The trial was a short one, both Pendleton and Kelly having recovered from their ordeal, gave clear evidence concerning the happenings on the April evening. Their testimony was confirmed by other witnesses and items found in the possession of the prisoners were displayed for the Grand Jury. The pawnbroker from Liverpool confirmed that the cousins had visited his premises on the Saturday morning in April to pawn the stolen watch.

The prisoners' hastily enlisted defence Counsel had a hopeless task and the inevitable Guilty verdict was duly recorded. This was fol-

Baron Wood and Justice Bayley resided at the Judges Lodging House, built in 1620, for the duration of the Lancaster Assizes

lowed by the passing of the death sentence on the pair of highway robbers who faced the same fate as six men hung at Lancaster in April 1817, for highway robbery.

By the time the Assizes were complete several others also faced the death sentence for offences ranging from housebreaking to stealing of a gelding. However, before he left the town the Hon. Baron Wood reprieved all the prisoners under sentence of death. The prisoners all faced transportation for life but at least Lancaster had for once been spared the spectacle of a public execution.

Chapter 14

Brutal Killing at The Brick Works

At the beginning of February 1898, George William Howe appeared at Manchester Assizes charged with the murder of John Keirby Pickup on New Year's Eve, 1897.

The story, as laid before the court by numerous witnesses, was that the 33-year-old Howe of Clarence Street, Burnley, had for a period of 12 months, up to the 27th of November of the previous year, been employed as a clay runner at the brick and tile works of Messrs. Brooks and Pickup and that his overseer had been the deceased man, John Pickup. Some complaint had been made as to Howe's work and regarding this as tantamount to a dismissal, he left his position.

Later he was reported to have said to a companion, "I am going to see Pickup about getting my work back. If ever my children want for bread, I will make Jack Pickup suffer for it. If my children have to starve, I will swing for Pickup".

Howe was unsuccessful in his application for reinstatement and nothing more was heard of him until eight o'clock in the morning on New Year's Eve, 1897. At that time he appeared at Burnley Police Station and made a sensational announcement, "At 6.30, this morning, I killed Jack Pickup. He has got me stopped for something I have never done. I have waited for him. I did it with a bit of a stick. No one saw me do it and no one saw me come away".

A police search followed immediately and, at a quiet spot on the tram lines of the brick and tile company, all the traces of a struggle were found. Blood was very much in evidence and a colliers stick with the knob broken off, as well as a battered signalman lantern smeared with blood, were discovered.

It appeared to have been the duty of the deceased to inspect all the tram lines before commencing work for the day, and the theory was that Howe, being thoroughly acquainted with this fact, surprised Pickup and assaulted him. When Howe left Pickup he was not dead, but managed to scramble to a gateway, where he was found by a railway watchman, bleeding from the head. His injuries were described as frightful and appeared to have been inflicted with the lamp or the heavy clogs which the prisoner was wearing. The unfortunate victim was removed to the Victoria Hospital, where he died some nine days later, without being able to make any significant communication to the police officers.

It was related that while in custody the prisoner had heard that Pickup was not dead when he left him, and he was alleged to have said, "If I had known he was not dead I would have gone back and given him some more. I had it in my crop for three weeks to do for him".

On another occasion he was said to have told his wife in the presence of a police officer, "I intended doing this a good bit. I did it with my stick".

The court heard that at the time of his arrest Howe's clothes bore traces of blood and that one of his clogs was covered with a considerable quantity of hair. The prosecution deduced from this that Howe had mercilessly kicked his victim on the head and face.

When the defence counsel presented their case they argued that without Howe's statements there would never have been a shred of evidence against him. Their argument was that had he intended to murder Pickup he would have armed himself with some other weapon than a stick, such as was used by all Lancashire colliers.

Mr Justice Wills however, was of the view that the case against the prisoner was, even without his own confession, a terribly strong one.

The jury were absent for about forty minutes considering their verdict and on their return the foreman announced that they were unanimous in their verdict that the prisoner had murdered Pickup.

Amid the silence of a crowded court His Lordship then assumed the black cap, and addressing Howe, said: "You have been found guilty upon the clearest evidence of a cruel and, I am afraid, deliberate murder upon this unfortunate man. You gave him no time to consider before he went to his last account – more mercy will be shown to you, and I implore you to make what use you can of it". The dread formula of the capital sentence then followed.

The prisoner who had followed the evidence with the closest attention, seemed to break down completely towards the close of the case. His black, dishevelled hair, pinched face and generally wretched appearance created a pitiable sight. Seeming to collapse altogether he had to be supported to the cells below by the warders.

The morning of Tuesday, February 22nd the day of Howe's execu-

BURNLEY TRAGEDY.

THE LAST SCENE.

EXECUTION THIS MORNING.

(BY OUR OWN REPORTER.)

This morning, George William Howe, of Burnley, paid the extreme penalty which the law demands for the murder of John Kirby Pickup.

The morning broke dull, foggy, and very cold, frost having everything hard within its grip. As early as seven o'clock one or two persons of morbid instinct had taken up position in the vicinity of the gaol. High above the walls, of which there loomed in clear view the big bare staff on which would soon flutter to the outer world intimation that the law had been carried into effect, watchers for the black flag steadily increased in number, and quite a crowd was present when at 7 30 the prisoners who had completed their term of punishment were liberated from gaol. There at the gates stood the prison missionary ready with a kindly greeting, and extending to each a little ticket by the production of which breakfast and assistance might be secured. In the majority of cases the coupons were screwed up and thrust away from sight, and the released prisoners, among whom women preponderated, hurried away out of sight or strolled across the road to join their assembled kindred spirits. Out came the right warders, hurrying away from the pile of buildings as though to stay there longer were intolerable. At 7 20 the chaplain of the prison, looking very pale but firm, entered the prison, to minister for the last time to the fated criminal.

Banner headline from the Lancashire Daily Post in February 1898.

tion broke dull, foggy and very cold with frost having everything within its grip. As early as seven o'clock one or two persons of morbid instinct had taken up position in the vicinity of Strangeways Gaol. By a quarter to eight various officials connected with the proceedings had entered the prison gates and by then the street outside was crowded for a considerable distance. The gathering was described as a "mixed assembly of low debased women, unemployed artisans and blackguardly specimens of the taproom loafer".

The doomed man's last moments were slowly running out as executioner Billington entered his cell with attendant warders to set about adjusting the pinioning bands. Howe was by now in terrible anguish but was bearing up heroically. Preserving a bearing of calm fortitude to the last, he had attention only for the solacing sentences that the chaplain in a low tone murmured, as two warders on either side walked with him to his doom. The Governor and the Sheriffs Officer headed the melancholy parade, while the executioner followed at the rear.

Once on the scaffold, executioner Billington carried out his duty and the bolt that sent Howe into eternity was drawn as the prison clock, with raucous clangour, rang out the hour. It was eight o'clock and the silence that reigned outside the prison gates was only broken when the crowd spotted the black flag being hoisted upwards in the dense, murky atmosphere of the February morning.

The subsequent inquest into the execution revealed that Howe had met his death with considerable fortitude and within a minute of the deed being performed, he was dead.

There was much sympathy for Howe who met his end in the city in which he was born. Most of his 33 years of life had been spent in Burnley although for part of his childhood he lived in Barnsley. Only once previously, had he been in the hands of the police and that was in 1896, when he was charged with deserting his family. He did not go to prison at the time, but was made to pay a fine. The official description of him was just under 5ft 6in tall, sallow complexion, dark brown hair, dark brown eyes. Before the tragic happenings that overtook him, he was said to weigh 11 stone, but by the day of reckoning he was some two stone lighter.

On the day of his execution he wrote a final letter to his wife and a copy of it was printed in that day's Lancashire Daily Post. Appearing next to a report of his passing, it was a sad sequel to the Burnley tragedy. The letter contained the following:

"...Thank God, I am totally prepared to meet my end, knowing that my prayers have been answered and that God will be merciful to me for this, the only one bad action during my 33 years on this earth. My dear wife, I hope you will bear up and try and face this hard world for the sake of the innocent children whom I am leaving behind. May God bless them, and may they always attend their Sunday school, which was always my wish. ... We must forgive those that trespass against us and I do not want to die with animosity against anyone. ...When I go to my doom this verse will be on my mind.

Just as I am Thou wilt receive,
Wilt welcome, pardon, cleanse, relieve,
Because Thy promise I believe.
Oh, Lamb of God I come.

... Dear wife, it is hard to say good-bye, but God bless you all, and may He let us all meet in heaven, for we have all to depart sooner or later. ... Never a better wife could a man have. Poor lass. Good-bye ... God have mercy on your broken-hearted husband,

George Howe"

Chapter 15

A Pilferer's Pitiful Plight

During the late summer of 1895 there was a lot of pilfering from the railway trucks in the sidings close by the North Western Railway station at Wigan. As a result the railway police officer, Detective Sergeant Osborne, enlisted the assistance of Detective Kidd from Manchester in order to increase their activities and catch those responsible.

The increased surveillance produced little reward until the night of September 28th. That night at around six o'clock three local colliers met in the New Inn, a public house situated on the south side of the railway. The three men William Kearsley, Elijah Winstanley and William Halliwell, spent over an hour in that place conversing and drinking and then resolved to go to the Fox Inn, another Wigan public house.

On their way there they made up their minds to go on the railway and see what they could get out of the trucks. On the right-hand side of the station platform there was a wall separating the line from the sidings and the goods yard. When they reached that point it was agreed that Halliwell would stay there and keep watch while the other two proceeded towards some trucks a little further down the sidings. Whilst Kearsley and Winstanley were pilfering the trucks the third man observed the railway policemen Osborne and Kidd coming along by the side of the wall.

Osborne caught sight of Halliwell and called out to him. Whereupon Halliwell called back and at the same time roused his two colleagues with the shout, "Heigh up, lads". Osborne at once rushed at Halliwell, caught him and a struggle commenced. In the meantime Kidd rushed round the corner of the wall towards the two men who had been in the railway trucks. What next took place by the side of the trucks was not seen by anyone, except for Kidd and the two men he confronted. The result, however, was that the detective was left dying by the side of the wagons, with stab wounds having been inflicted to his head and neck.

The scuffle between Detective Sergeant Osborne and Halliwell was a protracted one and only ended when Kearsley intervened, kicking the police officer whilst he struggled on the floor. By then the three colliers had regrouped and they made a hasty retreat.

Osborne eventually managed to recover enough to go down the track in search of Detective Kidd, finding him bleeding and almost devoid of life. His exertions had left him exhausted and after placing his colleague against a wall he collapsed. Eventually the two men were discovered and taken to the Infirmary. It was too late to attend to Kidd, but Osborne recovered quickly from his ordeal.

The three men went on to the Fox Inn after their escapade and as they sat drinking their ale Winstanley said, "I don't think the man I was 'agate' of will live, I stabbed him many a time". Soon after they were all arrested and Detective Osborne was most positive in his identification of them.

Towards the end of November the incident on the September evening was recalled at the Liverpool Assizes. Only two of the men faced a charge of murder, with William Halliwell being faced with the lesser charge of wounding. The key witness in the whole proceedings was Halliwell and he willingly related the night's events and the evidence suggested that Winstanley had been the main aggressor towards Detective Kidd.

The jury had little difficulty in reaching a verdict, taking only fifteen minutes to find both Winstanley and Kearsley 'Guilty' as charged. When asked if they had anything to say before sentence was passed, Winstanley replied, "It wasn't him (pointing to Kearsley). He never did it".

His Lordship, Mr Justice Collins, then assumed the black cap and said – "William Kearsley and Elijah Winstanley, after a patient hearing, you have both been found guilty of murder. Nothing now remains for me but to pass upon you the sentence of death".

The prisoners seemed filled with awe as the sentence was passed and at the conclusion of the solemnly pronounced words someone shouted out "Amen". For a moment or two the prisoners stood gazing at the Judge and as they were removed from the dock it was evident that Kearsley felt his position. Both men were then taken to Walton Gaol in a prison van with a small crowd watching as the van departed from the court.

The following morning Halliwell returned into court to be informed that no evidence would be offered against him – the 31-year-old collier then left the court a free man.

The court's verdict had created a lot of interest in Wigan and every effort was made to obtain a reprieve for the colliers who had resided in Kays Houses, Lower Ince, Wigan. The general feeling was that Kearlsey, who was in his mid-forties, had a good chance of a reprieve. He continued to claim his innocence and on the 10th day of December a Communication from Whitehall informed his solicitor that the capital sentence had been replaced by one of penal servitude for life. The news quickly circulated and his wife and family were reported as being overjoyed at the announcement.

The case of 31-year-old Winstanley was said to be still under review, but his hopes were dashed twenty four hours later. For Winstanley, who had been described as an intelligent, sober, industrious character, life was set to end on the scaffold. His wife and children were devastated by the news and the woman could not face the ordeal of paying him a final visit.

Other relatives and friends paid Winstanley a last visit and the party reported that the condemned man was deeply affected, shedding many a tear as he spoke of his wife and children.

The execution of Elijah Winstanley took place on the stroke of eight o'clock on Tuesday morning December the 17th, 1895. James Billington was the executioner assigned to the task and he completed his work efficiently. On a fine but cold morning, a large number of people had collected on the footpath opposite the prison and immediately after the execution the black flag was raised by one of the Walton Gaol warders. A number of spectators lingered until they saw Billington depart and in the meantime two printed notices had been fixed to the gaol gates stating that Winstanley had been duly executed.

Chapter 16

Martha Tries to Hide her Shame

During the month of September 1858, Joshua Bilcliff the landlord of the General Havelock public house in Stretford New Road, Manchester, had staying at his premises a young single woman, Martha Bilborough. The woman, who was 28 years of age, was a niece of the landlord and was in the fourth month of pregnancy. Being unmarried she was reluctant to reveal that she was with child and desperate to conceal her shame she made plans to have her pregnancy terminated.

To this end she made contact with a Doctor Auguste Wilhelm, a 29-year-old medical practitioner who hailed from Germany and who had recently moved to premises in Bury New Road. At his surgery Dr Wilhelm was assisted by a fellow countryman called Carl Stadtmuller, who was five years his junior.

During September, Martha Bilborough several times sent an old woman of her acquaintance to Dr Wilhelm's practice for medicines. Sometimes the messenger took a note and always she took money. Usually it was fifteen shillings or ten shillings, but on one occasion Dr Wilhelm had sent her back for extra cash. In return for the money the old woman was given a gill bottle of medicine. Sometimes it was mixed by the doctor and sometimes by his assistant.

Martha's health appeared to be in decline and when a neighbour, Mrs Wainwright, saw her crying she asked whatever was the matter. The young lady replied, "I have taken some medicine that makes me so ill, I can't take any more. I'll throw it away".

A few days later, on the last Sunday of the month between two and three o'clock in the afternoon, Martha walked down to Bury New Road and went to the premises occupied by Dr Wilhelm. She remained there until half past eleven o'clock when a cab was sent for and she was brought out of the house, looking very pale, and without wearing her bonnet. Mrs Wilhelm, got into the cab with her and carried her bonnet. Martha was taken home and went to bed immediately, her uncle observing that she looked very ill.

She continued poorly the next day but refused to allow another doctor to be sent for, only seeing Wilhelm and Stadtmuller, who called several times that day.

The uncle called on Mrs Wainwright to tend for the young woman and Martha told her that she had been taken ill while she was out on the Sunday afternoon. During the evening she exclaimed, "Oh! Mrs Wainwright, if you knew all". To which Mrs Wainwright commented, "Tell me, if it will ease you". Martha's response was, "I have done all this to hide shame". She then complained that her shoulder was sore and when Mrs Wainwright looked at it, she found a large black mark. To which Martha said, "That's were they laid hold of me ".

Despite the attention of Wilhelm and Stadtmuller who applied leeches and administered to her draughts and powder, the young woman was in decline. With Mrs Wainwright at her bedside the two medical practitioners often conversed in German and, after one earnest conversation, Stadtmuller was observed emptying the contents of a medicine bottle into a basin of dirty water and then putting the empty bottle into his pocket.

On the Tuesday evening Martha was suffering excruciating pain, and when her uncle called in a Dr Wilson, he discovered she had been cruelly treated. Shortly after the doctor had prescribed for her, she died.

After her death, Dr Wilson went to the Germans and accused them of attempting to procure an abortion. They denied the allegation and claimed that she had used violence upon herself. In fact, the girl's uncle had received from Dr Wilhelm a death certificate, signed by Carl Stadtmuller, which stated that death was caused by peritonitis and enteritis.

Dr Wilson subsequently made a post-mortem examination and found no signs of either disease. According to his findings death had been caused by inflammation produced by considerable lacerations, which the woman could not have done herself, and which must have been done by instruments. A later search of Dr Wilhelm's house led to the discovery of instruments capable of causing the lacerations and only used in the most extraordinary obstetric cases.

A subsequent inquest led to the two medical practitioners from Germany being committed to Kirkdale Gaol on a charge of wilful murder.

The trial took place in the middle of December 1858, with both men pleading Not Guilty to the charge laid before them. After the pleas had been made it was announced by the prosecution that, with His Lordship's agreement, they wished to have Stadtmuller acquitted. Agreement was given and the case against Stadtmuller was dropped.

Later in the day Carl Stadtmuller was called as a witness for the prosecution, and along with other witnesses, he recalled the last agonising days of Martha Bilborough's life. There was much evidence to condemn the doctor from Germany.

The jury, before they retired, were reminded by the Judge that if a person attempted to procure the abortion of a woman without lawful cause for doing so, they would be guilty of a highly unlawful act. They were also reminded that if a person for an unlawful purpose used a dangerous instrument, or medicine, or other means and thereby death ensued, that was murder. The options, the jury were told, were murder, manslaughter or acquittal.

In fact the jury consulted for only ten minutes, after which time they informed the Clerk of the Court that the prisoner was 'Guilty of murder', adding that they would have been glad to have brought in a manslaughter verdict – if the law would allow. His Lordship then indicated that the expression of their opinion would be forwarded to the proper quarters.

Breathless silence then prevailed; and Dr Wilhelm made no reply to the question as to what he had to say before sentence of death was passed. His Lordship then assumed the black cap and calmly delivered the dreaded sentence.

Over Christmas, Dr Wilhelm was confined in a condemned cell of Kirkdale Gaol and only the visits from his wife consoled him as he prepared for death. Mrs Wilhelm was greatly affected by her husband's situation and there was much sympathy for her. Amongst those who showed her kindness was a Mr Southern, the landlord of the Black Bull Inn, Kirkdale, who allowed her to stay at his house so that she may be close to the place of her husband's confinement.

As the days passed by Dr Wilhelm seemed resigned to his fate and was much surprised to learn that his sentence had been commuted to one of penal servitude for life. The news seemed to have struck him with dismay and apprehension. Writing to his sorrowing wife, he told her that he thought even death would have been sweeter than living with everlasting separation from her and their children.

Chapter 17

The Wreck of the "Ocean Monarch"

On Thursday, August 24th 1848, a calamity occurred in the River Mersey, near Liverpool, more terrific and melancholy than had been known within the limits of the port for many years.

The American ship "Ocean Monarch", of 1400 tons burden, left Liverpool early that Thursday morning with close on four hundred persons on board. Her progress through the channel was reported, and not long afterwards the sad news was received that she was in flames. This occasioned, in Liverpool, the greatest excitement and consternation, due to the fact that it was known she had on board such a large number of passengers.

Full particulars could not, however, be obtained until about five-thirty in the afternoon, when a yacht called the "Queen of the Ocean", returning from the Beamauris Regatta, brought the fearful intelligence that the "Ocean Monarch" had burnt to the water's edge and was a mere hulk. According to the yacht's owner, Mr Littledale, in the region of one hundred passengers had gone to a watery grave.

Mr Littledale had seen the "Ocean Monarch" at midday near the Great Ormshead where she suddenly put up her helm, as if to return to Liverpool, and hoisted a flag of distress. Flames could be seen bursting from her abaft and the yacht responded immediately by moving towards her. On nearing the ship the yacht lowered its life boat and by means of this thirty two persons were rescued from the dreadful fate which threatened them.

It appeared that at about twenty minutes before noon, smoke was seen to issue from the after part of the ship behind the steering wheel, under the captain's cabin. The alarm had been first given by the passengers in the second cabin, who ran upon deck crying out, "Fire, Fire!". A rush was immediately made to the decks and men, women and children ran about in a state of frenzy, crying, wringing their hands and supplicating for help. Water was called for by the captain and a few buckets were thrown in the area where the fire appeared to rage.

The *Ocean Monarch* presented a scene of despair

The water did little to dampen the blaze and the flames began to advance rapidly in the after part of the ship. The mate left the wheel and it appeared almost hopeless to make any attempt to subdue the flames. The fire progressed at a fearful rate and all those on board headed for the fore part of the ship. Some of them got upon the bowsprit, the jib-booms, into the rigging, or any place, in fact, that presented the fairest chance of escape.

Many, driven to despair, jumped overboard and committed themselves to the deep; they floated for a short time and then sank to rise no more. It was reported that the captain left the vessel soon after the fire broke out and was not seen again.

Soon after the appearance of Mr Littledale's yacht, the Brazilian steam frigate, "Affonso", arrived at the scene and numbers of the unfortunate people who had escaped from the burning vessel, were picked up and taken on board. Many of them had been clinging to pieces of wood, spars and anything that offered a hope of relief in their perilous position.

When Mr Littledale had arrived the flames had been bursting with immense fury from the stern and centre of the vessel. So great being the heat in those parts that the passengers, men, women and children crowded to the fore part of the vessel, their piercing heart rendering shrieks for aid being carried by the breeze across the blue waters. In their maddened despair women jumped overboard with their off-spring in their arms and sank to rise no more. Men followed their wives in frenzy and were lost. Groups of men, women and children threw themselves into the water, in the vain hope of self-preservation, but the waters closed over many of them forever.

The flames continued to rage with increased fury. In a few minutes the mizen mast went overboard – a few minutes more and the main mast shared the same fate, only the fore mast remained. The passengers and crew crowded still further forward, to the jib-boom they clung in clusters as thick as they could pack – even one lying over another. At length the fore mast went overboard, snapping the fastenings of the jib-boom which, with its load of human beings, dropped into the water amidst the most heart-rendering screams, both from those on board and those who were fallen into the water. Some of the poor creatures were able to again reach the vessel and cling by ropes, others floated away on spars, but many met with a watery grave.

The frigate "Affonso" rendered the most effective service to the unfortunate crew and passengers of the "Ocean Monarch". She anchored immediately to windward and close to the burning vessel, with a rope made fast to the troubled ship her boats were able to go backwards and forwards with great facility and by this means large numbers were saved.

Shortly afterwards the "Prince of Wales" steamer, en-route to Bangor arrived on the scene as did the "New World" packet ship bound for New York. Both vessels sent boats to the rescue of the troubled passengers and helped to reduce the fearful death toll.

All the sufferers, the greater portion of whom were emigrants from the South of Ireland, lost their luggage, clothes and everything which they possessed. Many of them, when landed, were nearly naked and had borrowed coats, jackets and other articles of wearing apparel in order to protect themselves from the cold. Throughout the Thursday afternoon and evening the survivors were landed at Liverpool and they were given every attention which sympathy, pity and hospitality could bestow.

Over the next few days the extent of the disaster came to light and the statistics made harsh reading. The "Ocean Monarch" had sailed with 396 persons aboard, made up of 322 steerage passengers, 32 first and second cabin passengers and 42 crew. In all 218 were accounted for and 178 were reported as missing. The "Affanso" was reported to

Seaman Frederick Jerome came to the aid of a dozen helpless women and children

have rescued 156 people and 32 people were indebted to Mr Littledale and his yacht the "Queen of the Ocean".

Amongst those who distinguished themselves and earned praise for their efforts were numerous officers and seamen of the "Affonso" steam frigate.

One man who earned particular praise was Frederick Jerome, seaman of the ship "New World", who exerted himself notably towards the close of the melancholy scene. He came to the aid of a dozen helpless women and children who remained on the burning wreck. Paralysed with fear, they were totally incapable of helping themselves by descending from the tottering bowsprit to the boats which waited in the midst of the heavy seas.

Observing their predicament, Frederick Jerome made his way through the sea and the wreck, and with a line in his hand succeeded in lowering them safely into boats. He himself being the last to leave the ill-fated vessel.

Some of the passengers severely censored the conduct of the captain, whom they described as at once losing his coolness and composure. Stating that instead of giving those directions which were essential for the safety of the passengers, he had thrown himself overboard and left them to their fate.

Other passengers and members of the crew distinctly contradicted such a statement remarking that Captain Murdoch maintained his presence of mind to the last and that he did not leave the ship until the flames compelled him to do so, as the only means of escape, adding that if the passengers had generally followed his directions, many more would have been saved.

The Chief Mate of the "Ocean Monarch" in a letter addressed to "The Times" expressed the following observations :- "As to the origin of the fire, I differ from a published statement I have seen. There were no wooden ventilator on board the ship; the ventilators were of iron. The fire originated, in my opinion, from smoking amongst the steerage passengers; the night before several pipes were taken from them. The fire was instantaneous; five minutes after it was discovered the whole stern of the ship was in flames. The cargo consisted of iron, dry goods, salt and earthenware, the latter being packed in crates stuffed with straw".

With a view of obtaining a complete muster of the survivors so that their names might be recorded, a meeting was held on the Sunday in the offices of Messrs. Haraden in Waterloo Road. In all, 150 persons attended to make record and although private charity had in the meantime provided clothing for many, a majority of the poor creatures were in the most wretched and destitute condition.

One poor woman who was present had lost not less than five of her children; and it was pitiable to hear the recital of personal loss and peril which each poor sufferer had to tell.

The survivors were informed that two more ships were sailing in the following week and places were available for them if they so desired. Great numbers however, declined the offer having been terrified by what they had observed and suffered and the following day they appeared at the Waterloo Road offices for the return of their passage money.

During the following week, almost every tide brought up to the Blackpool coast quantities of wreck, consisting chiefly of planks and spars. From the charred appearance of the timbers it was evidently portions of the ill-fated "Ocean Monarch". On the Wednesday evening the wind, which had previously been veering from the south-east to south, moved round to the west and the consequence was that a number of bodies were cast upon the west coast, at or near Blackpool. A number of inhabitants assembled to secure the bodies and convey them ashore for interment. Due to discolouration and disfigurement it was difficult to give a definite description of each. The shores at Lytham, Fleetwood, Pilling and Blackpool all had victims cast upon them and the local press gave descriptions in an attempt to aid relatives in identifying their lost ones.

One female was washed up near Lytham lighthouse. She had on a light coloured dress and in her pocket was found a shipping ticket, headed 'Harden and Co's, American Packet Office, 60 Waterloo Road, Liverpool. The "Ocean Monarch", 1400 tons register, bound to Boston, sailed the 24th August, passage money £10' (for the steerage).

The names entered in the ticket were, James Mentagh, 24; Mrs Mentagh and Infant, 20; Jane Mentagh, 18.

Many of the victims were identified as each tide brought more bodies to the shores and the unidentified were placed in good coffins and interred in the local church yards.

Chapter 18

Stabbings on a Saturday Night

On the second Saturday night of April 1853, three young men who were factory operatives in the employ of Messrs. Catterall & Co. of Catterall, and fellow lodgers at the house of Lucy Singleton of the same place, went together to the Horns Inn public house at Garstang. The three of them, William Pendlebury, John Wilding (alias Blackburn Jack) and Thomas Rogerson had a gill of ale each, after which Wilding proposed that they adjourn to the Rose and Crown Inn, situated at the foot of the town on the road to Catterall.

With an outpouring of generosity Wilding promised to pay for the ale if his friends went with him. Once inside the Rose and Crown Pendlebury ordered a pint of ale asking Wilding to pay for it as agreed. Wilding refused and when pressed on the matter became irritated. His annoyance was even more apparent a couple of minutes later when he threw a glass of ale, given him by Rogerson, into the fire.

In an attempt to defuse the situation Pendlebury told Wilding that he would release him from his promise, if he would pay for a pennyworth of tobacco. He agreed and his handing over of the tobacco seemed to ease the tension.

The three had been in the Rose and Crown about half an hour and just before eleven o'clock they rose and left the house, in order to proceed to Catterall. No sooner had they got outside the inn than Wilding attacked Rogerson and dealt him several kicks. Rogerson then ran to join Pendlebury for protection and the two of them proceeded along the road.

On arriving at the foot of a hill, not far from their lodgings, they sat down on the copse to allow Wilding an opportunity of joining them, so that they might all go home together. While waiting there they were passed by a clogger called William Benson, who was on his way back home to Garstang. When he asked what they were doing they replied that they were waiting for 'Blackburn Jack'.

A little nearer to Garstang, Benson came upon Wilding who said that two men had robbed him of half a sovereign and ill-used him, adding, "Had you been one of them I would have rammed this into you", showing him an open clasp knife. Benson told him it was improper to carry such a weapon, but taking no notice Wilding continued on his way.

Carrying on towards Garstang, Benson was surprised a few minutes later by the re-appearance of Wilding, who had the knife still open in his hand. The weapon was covered with blood and Wilding, in an apparent agitated state, repeatedly said, "I have stabbed one man twice, and another man once". Then after uttering several incoherent statements Wilding requested Benson to go with him to the police station and he accordingly accompanied him there.

When Wilding entered the police station with the open knife in his hand, he told the duty officer, PC Murrow, that he had stabbed two men, murdering one of them and leaving the other not far from dead. Straight away the constable and Sergeant Brownell, who was also on late duty, took up a lantern and accompanied Wilding to the place where the deed had been committed. The spot was at the foot of a hill called Bowgrave, some three hundred yards from the Rose and Crown public house. On the road there, Wilding, who was intoxicated and very excited, said, "I left them lying there; they said they would do for me sometime, and I was determined to do for them tonight".

On arriving at Bowgrave they found William Pendlebury, lying dead in a pool of blood some five or six yards in length. There was a terrible gash from which the blood had flowed in the inside part of his thigh. The body of Pendlebury was at once taken to the Rose and Crown and Wilding was taken to the lock up.

Meanwhile, Thomas Rogerson the other victim of Wilding's aggression, was on his way back to the lodgings in Catterall. He had been stabbed in the back but his wound was not life threatening and as soon as he returned home he gave information of the occurrence. Two men whom he had alerted rushed to the scene of the incident and arrived at the same time as Wilding and the police officers.

After receiving medical attention, Rogerson was able to give an account of the incident that had left him injured and his friend dead. He stated that after they got up from the copse, Wilding began being awkward with him again and punched him on the leg. To which action Pendlebury reacted by grabbing hold of Wilding and saying, "He is not thy equal, if thou will start, start of thy equals".

Wilding retaliated by shoving Pendlebury and striking him with his knife. Crying out, "Oh, Tom he has stuck me," the unfortunate Pendlebury slumped to the ground, falling upon his belly. In the next

The night of tragedy began at the Horns Inn public house

instant Rogerson was under threat, as Wilding lunged toward him. Rogerson stooped as his assailant aimed a blow at him and the knife was run into his back.

According to Rogerson, Wilding then ran off towards Garstang, leaving his two victims lying in the lane.

The trial for wilful murder by twenty-six-year-old John Wilding took place at the Lancaster Summer Assizes held in August 1853, before Mr Justice Wightman. Not surprisingly much depended on the testimony of the 17-year-old Thomas Rogerson, who related the sorry affair.

The Defence Counsel pointed out that the whole case seemed to rest upon the testimony of one man, claiming that inconsistencies had been proved in his evidence and that he had reasons for not rendering a faithful version of the night's transaction.

When His Lordship summed up, he told the jury that he suspected that they had not heard all that had taken place, pointing out that they must be satisfied that the prisoner had a deliberate intention to take away life, before they could convict him of such a grave charge.

The jury, after their deliberations, returned into court with a verdict of 'not guilty' on the wilful murder charge, but 'guilty' on the count of manslaughter.

Mr Justice Wightman then addressed Wilding, telling him that he had been convicted of manslaughter under circumstances of great aggravation. The jury had given him the benefit of reasonable doubt as to his intention to cause the death of William Pendlebury. The fact that he might have received great provocation was not a justification, but had reduced the offence. His Lordship then concluded by stating that this was one of the many crimes resulting from intoxicating drinks and the fact that it involved the use of a deadly weapon meant it must be severely punished. John Wilding was then informed that his sentence was one of transportation for twenty years.

The crowded transportation ship awaited the convicted criminal John Wilding

Chapter 19

An Impostor's Deceitful Trail

Amongst the calendar of crimes that Mr Justice Park had to preside over at the Lancaster Assizes of March 1830, was a case of highway robbery at Scotforth, near Lancaster.

The crime was said to have been committed on the 23rd February of that year and the prosecutor was Robert Stanley, who had been on his way to Lancaster. The court heard that he had been stopped on the road by a woman, who asked for charity from him. Immediately after her were two men, one of whom struck him a blow on the head, which knocked him senseless on the ground and he remembered no more.

Accused of the desperate highway robbery were Paul Rigby, aged 47, John Grimes, aged 62 and Mary Grimes, aged 27. The three listened intently as it was related that Robert Stanley, said to hail from Oswestry, in Shropshire, had been left for dead. He had been discovered by a local man, William Clark who had found him quite cold and fastened to a gate. With the help of others he took the distraught man to a neighbouring house, where his neck cloths were removed, along with several coils of wire and pack thread, which had been twisted tight around his throat.

The landlord of the Boot and Shoe public house at Scotforth, identified the prisoners as the threesome who had visited his inn at around seven o'clock on the night in question, while nine-year-old Titus Slater told how he had overhead John Grimes say to the woman, "We are just right for killing a man, we have plenty of wires in the basket".

Other witnesses spoke of seeing the prisoners the night the assault was committed, and it was claimed that the woman had wire in her basket whilst they were at the Boot and Shoe public house. In their defence the accused claimed that the wire in their possession was in fact used for the purpose of cleaning bottles.

The prosecution emphasised the point that if Robert Stanley had not been discovered at the time he was, he would in all probability have died.

Scotforth's ancient Boot & Shoe Inn visited by the accused

Robert Stanley related that he had been very ill and sick after his ordeal and told the gathering he had been robbed of two £5 Bank of England Notes, silver coins to the value of 5 shillings, a silver watch, a gold seal, a silver pencil case, a key and a parcel containing a shirt and two pairs of stockings.

In all, a great deal of circumstantial evidence was stacked up against the accused, and although they protested their innocence, the Jury delivered a Guilty verdict in all the cases. The matter of sentencing was deferred for a couple of days at which time Mr Justice Park ordered the prisoners back into the dock.

He told them that they had been convicted of one of the most cruel kind of robberies ever perpetrated. But for the merciful interference of the providence of God, the young man, whom they robbed and left tied with wires to a gate in a state of suffocation, must certainly have lost his life. His Lordship then passed sentence of death on all three, holding out little hope of mercy.

Particulars of the case were reported in the newspapers and the crime created particular interest to the inhabitants of Oswestry. The general consensus in that area was that no such person as Robert

The Assizes at Lancaster Castle in March 1830 included a peculiar case of highway robbery

Stanley resided in their midst, and the case brought back to mind a similar incident that had occurred at Wolverhampton in February 1829. On that occasion a similar highway robbery had been reported and brought to trial. A man calling himself Robert Fisher, a native of Oswestry, had been found in a situation similar to that of Robert Stanley. He had claimed that on a dark foggy February night he had been attacked on the highway and robbed of money and possessions. Inquiries were at that time made at Oswestry, and the conclusion drawn was that no one of his name or description had been resident there. However, before the complete detection of this artful impostor could be made, he disappeared from the scene.

Recognising the striking similarities between the two cases, a number of the principal inhabitants of Oswestry immediately communicated their information to Mr Justice Park, who at once granted a temporary respite to the condemned convicts. A police officer from Oswestry was sent to Lancaster in the hope that he could help to unravel the mystery. He was familiar with the impostor Fisher and he hoped to be able to verify that he and Stanley were in fact the same.

However, within a couple of days of the trial finishing, Stanley had made his departure from Lancaster; the description the constable received however seemed to precisely correspond with his own description of Fisher.

It was believed that Stanley had left Lancaster on a coach bound for Liverpool and by a strange coincidence the chaplain of the jail at Lancaster received the following letter on the 20th of March, bearing a Liverpool postmark:

"Sir,- I hav rote this to say that the two men and woman wo are condend for robing mister Stanle are inosent of the crim for it was me and another that robed him. - We folled him from Gaston and had no chonc to get by him in the public loune at gogat - We thote to stop him before it was too late - We got inside the Gate and waited for him but the woman ump begt of him lik to stoppt us - We saw the 3 pris-oners go and stopt to make water at the gat they was dronk quarilin at that time - th mon that swore to the glons has done rong - You will be convinced that it was not them by riting to the clirgyman of Wroxton near to maidstone in Kent for he is a Justis too - We robed a man there and tid him with wire the same but not to a gate about crismas last - We robed 1 to between ashby de la souse and Derby sometime before but we did not ty him - if you will rite to these plases you will find from this that they poor foks ar as much innocent as you - We hav robed 8 men altogether but will not rob no more for we have got money anof to carry us out of the Country and that is Hall we wanted for we cud not get work in this - the money and things my pardner took to hirlund soon after - if this is not true and I ever fixed any of the prisoners i wish i may sink to the bottom and find myself over last in hell torment so help me good god - i dur not put my name."

The officiating Clergeyman at Lancaster Castle.

Received 20 March, 1830; Liverpool post mark. 18 March, 1830

Prior to the trial at Lancaster Assizes, the case against the prisoners had been heard by the Magistrates and at that stage Robert Stanley had given the name of the Rev Thomas Venables, Minister at Oswestry, to vouch for him. Admiral Tatham, who presided at that hearing, addressed a letter accordingly, and on the 6th of March he received the following reply on a letter with an Oswestry postmark.

Oswestry, March 5th, 1830

"Sir, - I received yours of the 2nd instant and am sorry to hear of poor Stanley's misfortune - he is not known to me in person - but I have made inquiry and find him to bear a very good character since his residence in this town. He is but in a small way of business but is considered very industrious.

I have the honour to be, Sir,

Your mo. obt. huml. Sevt.

THOS. VENABLES

P.S. I should wish Stanley to call on me when he returns."

The police officer from Oswestry returned to his home to report the developments to the interested inhabitants. Within days he contacted Mr Justice Park again, to state that there was no such person of the name of Thomas Venables residing in Oswestry.

The learned Judge, who was by then attending to matters at the York Assizes, acted immediately on the information received and transmitted a communication to save the lives of the prisoners. They had protested their innocence throughout their ordeal and fortunately for them, the alertness of the residents of Oswestry had prevented a cruel miscarriage of justice. At the trial a couple of points had appeared favourable to the prisoners, one being that when searched a couple of hours after the incident none of the stolen property had been found in their possession, and the other being that the woman, when arrested, had been wearing a grey cloak and black bonnet instead of a dark cloak and light coloured bonnet, as described by Stanley. These facts had been brushed aside at the trial and in the light of the later developments they gained much greater significance, helping to exonerate the three people whose lives were almost lost on the testimony of a deceitful trickster.

Chapter 20

Slaughter of The Servants

On Saturday the 26th of April 1817, Mr Littlewood, a grocer who resided in a genteel house at Pendleton, some two miles from Manchester, left his home accompanied by his wife to attend to business at his shop in Manchester. He left his house in the safe keeping of his aged housekeeper Margaret Marsden, aged 75 and a young domestic servant, Hannah Partington, aged 20.

That afternoon around about one o'clock a servant girl from a nearby house passed the kitchen window of Mr Littlewood's home on her way to obtain some water from his pump. Looking into the kitchen she saw a man seated at the kitchen table.

Shortly afterwards the shutters, which hung on the inside of the kitchen window, were closed and according to village neighbours three men were observed coming out of the front gate of the premises, which led onto the busy turnpike road. Two of the men were seen to have a bundle in their arms.

Later that afternoon another servant girl from the neighbourhood called at the house to see Hannah Partington. The doors were locked and many of the blinds down and after peering under the kitchen blind and seeing the housekeeper reclined in an armed chair, apparently asleep, she decided to leave, not wishing to disturb her rest.

Shortly before seven o'clock, some three hours after her first visit, the servant girl returned. All was as before and the doors remained locked. The situation aroused her suspicions and looking again through the window she saw the housekeeper, who now appeared to be slumped forward in her chair and had a lifeless look about her.

The girl immediately raised the alarm and a number of neighbours were soon on the scene. A ladder was brought in order to effect an entry and as this was being done Mr Littlewood appeared, his day's work complete. Once inside the party made their way to the kitchen and there a terrible sight awaited them. Slumped in her usual chair was the aged housekeeper and at her feet was the mangled body of the 20-year-old domestic girl.

The murder of the housekeeper had been effected by means of a large iron poker, which was found bent and bloody near her body. While the young girl had been butchered with an iron cleaver.

The house had been plundered of £160, which Mr Littlewood kept in an upstairs room, gold and silver plate, a watch, some linen and various other articles.

Immediately a great investigation got underway in a bid to find the perpetrators of the dreadful crime. Many of the villagers were able to assist and they recalled seeing a number of strangers in Pendleton that afternoon. Among them were said to be three members of a family by the name of Ashcroft, two brothers and a son. They had lived in the village a number of years before and were familiar to the locals.

As a result of the enquiries six men were apprehended by Sunday evening and among them were the three Ashcrofts. Further investigations eliminated one of the suspects and when the trial took place in September 1817, five men stood accused. They were James Ashcroft, the elder, David Ashcroft his brother, James Ashcroft, son of the first named, William Holden and John Robinson.

The Friday morning trial took place at Lancaster Assizes before Lord Chief Baron Richards. It began at 8 o'clock and the court was so excessively crowded that it was with the utmost difficulty that the Counsel could gain access to their seats.

No expense was spared on the part of the prosecution to elucidate the horrible murders and in all twenty six witnesses were examined on the part of the prosecution. A model of the premises was exhibited in court and also drawings and plans of the house and adjoining grounds.

Witnesses testified to having seen David Ashcroft, the young James Ashcroft and another person, believed to be William Holden, leaving the house through the garden gate at around the time the murders were committed. While the servant girl who visited the water pump was said to have positively identified William Holden as the man she observed inside the kitchen.

Though no part of the stolen property which could be identified was traced to any of the other prisoners, it was stated that property corresponding with that lost by Mr Littlewood was proved to be in the possession of the young James Ashcroft. It was testified that a few hours after the murders were committed he had appeared at a gaming place in Manchester with a handful of gold and a great number of notes, though the same morning he had been so poor as not able to pay a debt of three shillings. Upon the person of David Ashcroft, it was stated were found five one pound Bank of England notes, and seven and a half guineas in gold.

At this stage the evidence submitted applied less to the elder Ashcroft than the other prisoners, but then the prosecution turned to a man who had been confined at the time Ashcroft was being investigated. This man, who shared his prison cell, claimed that Ashcroft confided in him. He told the court that James Ashcroft the elder had told him he acted as look out, while the others burgled the house and if anybody had approached the house he had arranged to signal to them, by placing his hat on a thorn bush close to the hedge where he was concealed. A local butcher was also called and he gave evidence of the appearance of the elder Ashcroft in his shop that day.

In all the case for the prosecution lasted until four o'clock and at that point the prisoners were called upon for their defence. The defence case lasted for just one hour as a handful of witnesses spoke on their behalf. Not denying their presence in Pendleton on the day of the tragedy, the prisoners attempted to distance themselves from the scene of the crime. All of them had been confronted during the investigation with the bodies of the murdered women and all claimed innocence in regard to the deaths.

The elder Ashcroft claimed that the evidence of his former cell mate was a complete fabrication. Another witness claimed that James Ashcroft, the younger, had exhibited Bank of England notes and gold in a public house in Manchester a couple of days prior to the murders.

It was next the turn of His Lordship to sum up the day's proceedings and in all he addressed the jury for close on two hours. As soon as His Lordship had concluded, the jury turned round in their box, and after some three minutes of deliberation the foreman was ready to deliver their verdict.

The verdict was Guilty against all the prisoners, except John Robinson, whom no evidence had been submitted against. The scene was immediately one that beggared all description. All the convicted men, as if with one voice, vehemently protested their innocence, and the wife of the younger Ashcroft rent the court with the most piercing shrieks, which produced the most distressful feeling in every person present.

Eventually, some degree of composure and silence was restored and the Clerk of the Court addressed the prisoners, asking them why judgment of death should not be passed upon them. Each of the four men claimed their innocence addressing the court in the following terms:

James Ashcroft, the elder said:

"Because so many lies have been told of us, I pray that God Almighty would even now send down the angels of these murdered women to testify our innocence".

David Ashcroft said:

"There have been so many perjured witnesses examined amongst us, that we had no means of defending ourselves. We are innocent of this murder, and I pray to God that it may be revealed who has done this cruel killing."

James Ashcroft, the younger said:

"I am going to die for this and I die innocent, and I thank God for it. I hope you will be kind to my poor wife and dear children, whom I leave thus friendless in the world."

William Holden said:

"Yes, there is a God who will judge this cause again, and those who now sit in judgement upon us. I am innocent as a child of murder."

There was then a general loud and vehement cry from all the prisoners, "Yes we are all innocent and shall die declaring our innocence". The elder James Ashcroft with the most enthusiastic vehemence, extending his arms as high as possible, and waving a handkerchief, exclaimed in an elevation of voice which reverberated throughout the court, "Glory be to God! We are innocent, and we shall die innocent".

The judge, who appeared evidently distressed by this strange and unusual scene, said, "Prisoners, you behave in a manner very unbecoming your unhappy situation".

Silence being restored, he then proceeded to pass sentence of death upon each of them, remarking on his perfect satisfaction with regard to the verdict of the jury. He told them they would be executed on Monday next, and their bodies given to the surgeons for dissection.

On the Saturday morning two other criminals, John Nuttall and Henry Schofield, who had been convicted of murder earlier in the week, were executed. They were both said to acknowledge the guilt of their crimes and to have conducted themselves in a respectable manner during their final hours.

The murderers from Pendleton showed no such remorse and as they awaited their sentence they continued to protest their innocence. Public curiosity was so great that an hour before the time of

The crowds made their way in great numbers through the streets of old Lancaster to witness the mid-day executions (19th century engraving)

execution the churchyard and ground adjoining was crowded more than on any former occasion. Shortly after noon, the executioner was seen preparing to fulfil his office, as he appeared on the platform. He was followed by William Holden, who addressed the spectators with great feeling, claiming he was as innocent of the crime as an unborn baby. Next came David Ashcroft, who was unwilling to be tied up until he had spoken to the crowd. He began by informing the spectators, "You are all here assembled to see four innocent men suffer, and I bless the Lord for it, there is not a man here who is not as guilty of the murder as we are".

Next to appear on the scaffold was James Ashcroft the younger, who was followed by his father, who kissed his son and conversed with him in an inaudible voice.

With the four men tied up and awaiting their fate, the hangman left the platform. As he did so the criminals began to sing a verse from Watts' hymn: "My days of praise shall ne'er be past, While life, or thought, and being last —" at the word "thought" in the second line, their voices faltered, the drop fell and they were left suspended. An awful pause followed, such as had not been witnessed on any former occasion. After hanging the usual time the bodies were cut down and delivered to the surgeons for dissection.

It had been a busy weekend for Lancaster Castle's resident executioner, Edward Barlow, who had followed up nine executions at the Spring Assizes with a further six after the latest judicial proceedings. Burglary, highway robbery, uttering of forged notes and murder had all been punished by the taking of the wrongdoer's life.

Postscript: In the book 'Time-Honoured Lancaster', it states that for twelve months the popular excitement knew no bounds, everyone being satisfied that these unfortunate men were all innocent of the crimes with which they were charged. The old files of the Lancaster Gazette, 1842-5 state that twenty six years later, a man confessed while on his death-bed, that he was the real criminal.

Chapter 21

A Frenzy of Fear at The Colosseum

On the second Friday of October 1878, the popular Colosseum Theatre, in Liverpool, which was used as a Music Hall, was filled with 4,000 people all eager to witness the farewell benefit for the comic singer Fred Coyne. Every available seat was taken in the galleries and over 2,000 people filled the pit and the passageways for the 'first house' which began at seven o'clock that evening.

The first part of the entertainment went along without interruption and after an hour Fred Coyne made his appearance on stage, rendering the song, 'You don't mean what I mean'. Before the song was completed a scuffle broke out in a corner of the pit, immediately under the gallery, and the disturbance quickly developed into a free fight. The disturbance could not be seen from every part of the house and a great deal of excitement followed when the cry of "Fire!" was raised.

Upon the cry the vast audience was seized with a frenzy of fear. A sudden impulse seemed to impel men, women and children to frantically make for the staircases, doors and windows. All efforts by those officials present to prevent the deathly rush were to no avail. The women and children shrieked, the men cried for help and the crowd continued pouring from all the places – the galleries, pit and passages – to the staircases.

People were trampling each other under foot; they clambered down the pillars, tore away the benches, jumped upon the stage, and fought desperately to vacate the building that they believed to be in flames. As the people rushed from the upper galleries to the narrow staircase, they were implored to stay calm. Some took the advice but the vast majority were far too excited to heed any warnings. Their fears being heightened when it was realised that the door leading from the galleries to the main staircase was closed and bolted. The crowd pressed frantically against it with some men attempting to kick through the door panels, but all their efforts to force the door were futile. Such was the pressure of the crowd that a terrible struggle for life was developing.

Efforts were made to get the crowd away from the door, where they

The Colosseum Theatre was a scene of panic in October 1878 *(Illustrated London News)*

were trampling each other to death, to reach the space behind, but most of them continued to madly clamour and struggle at the door to get out. Officials tried to pacify them but the alarm continued and from the shrieks and cries at the doorway and on the staircase there was no doubt that many unfortunate creatures were being crushed to death or suffocated.

At this point several of the artists appeared on the stage and endeavoured to pacify the audience by shouting, "No fire! No fire!" At that very moment an additional light was thrown on the stage from the gas lights in the wings. The crowd thought this confirmed their fear of the place being ablaze and fresh cries of "Fire, fire!" were raised. Immediately a rush was made for the stage by those in the pit who had not been able to get to the doors. The seats and benches were broken, the people clambered down and in a very short time the stage was crowded with an excited multitude. It was at once made clear to them that their alarm was unfounded and they were got out as soon as possible through the stage door in Manesty Lane.

Whilst this was going on, hundreds more were engaged in a frightful struggle to reach the narrow staircase that led to the street. The main entrance was guarded by a double door that opened internally and against this the crowd exerted tremendous pressure.

Fortunately the fire brigade arrived quickly and after ascertaining the fire alarm was a false one, they set about restoring calm. The brigade rushed to the main entrance and in finding it completely blocked, took their hatchets from their belts and beat back those who were crushing down the stairs. Once inside the theatre, the superintendent of the brigade, Mr Copland, realised that a great number had been trampled to death, and that others were dying. He at once ordered medical assistance and made plans to convey the injured to hospital. The cries of the maimed and those who were endeavouring to escape were described as being hideous and piteous. Some five hundred were still in the pit making the most violent efforts to get out.

At this point Mr Copland made himself heard saying, "Listen to me, my people. I assure you there is no fire. For gracious sake sit still and let us get out those who are injured. Already many have been killed; don't make a foolish attempt to get out. There is no cause for alarm". The crowd seemed to heed the fire officer's words and the panic began to subside.

Amongst those who rushed to give medical aid was a Manchester surgeon who had been drinking in the Colosseum Vaults when the alarm was raised and he gave the following account: – "I ran out, and found at the Paradise Street door of the Theatre a mass of human beings, packed one on top of the other like herrings in a barrel, right to the top of the doorway. The crowd outside, in spite of the remonstrations of the police, persisted in trying to pull out the poor creatures who were at the bottom; but of course it was impossible to extricate them in consequence of the weight upon them. I have no doubt that in this manner many limbs were pulled out. Nothing could be done until the firemen arrived, and then they went in by another door and pulled off those who were on the top. I went in myself to get out the dead and the dying. I got the police to clear out the crowd, and then we set to work. There were heaped together men, women and children. It was an unutterably ghastly spectacle. Some had their heads twisted under their bodies and their necks broken.

We first separated the dead from the dying. I tried the pulses of those who were lying there, and those I found to be dead we laid in a row at one side. The clothes of the living I tore apart and set the policemen to work to induce artificial respiration. As soon as possible the sufferers were placed in cabs and sent off to the hospital. I had not a soul to assist me – no other doctors could be found.

Mr Griffiths, of the Colosseum Vaults, provided brandy for all who required it, and by administering this stimulant, I restored consciousness in several cases. I, myself, was treated very roughly in the frantic crowd and am bruised all over".

The scene in the Royal Infirmary, Liverpool where a small room had been set aside for the reception of the dead, was most appalling. Stretched on the floor in all the stillness and hush of death lay no fewer than 33 bodies. Most of the bodies seemed to be those of strong labouring men, dock labourers, navvies and porters. The greater part had their mouths wide open, which showed that the poor souls had been gasping for breath at the last moment as they were suffocated by the pressure of the maddened throng.

Altogether 37 persons were taken to the Royal Infirmary and the four who did not succumb to their injuries, were tended to on the wards. The four were John Ball, a labourer, suffering from contusions of the legs; Simon Dorryall, a seaman, contusions of the side; Robert Lindop who had a wound to his hand and James Vincent, a fat man, who was so shocked that he was unable to speak.

The death toll was increased to 37 when it was ascertained that both the Northern and Southern Hospitals, had received two victims of the catastrophe. It was also reported that the disaster had left eight widows and twenty children had lost a parent.

While lamenting the tragedy, Mr Goodman, the manager of the Theatre, was quick to point out that during the previous 18 months the music hall had been visited by 30,000 people weekly, without any accidents occurring.

On the following Monday night the Theatre was re-opened with a variety performance of song and dance. At seven o'clock the curtain was raised and there were about 1,500 persons in the house, chiefly lads and lasses of the lower classes. Mr Goodman stepped forward and addressed a few words to the audience. He told those gathered that he deeply deplored the terrible calamity that had taken place. His concern, he revealed, was to relieve those who had suffered and with that object in mind he would give the proceeds of two night's entertainment for the relief of the relatives of the deceased. He told those gathered that he had opened that night to show the place was safe and that the accident would not have occurred if those present had not lost their heads. He then thanked them all for their attendance and the performance proceeded.

Chapter 22

Slum Sister's Arsenic Atrocities

On a dull overcast October afternoon in 1883, amidst the slums of Ascot Street in Liverpool, the family of Thomas Higgins gathered by his coffin, awaiting the arrival of the hearse to convey his mortal remains to their last resting place. Amongst the mourners was his wife Margaret, a charwoman in her early forties, and her 55-year-old sister Catherine Flanagan.

Thomas Higgins had been wed just a few months and his illness had been very brief and had arisen suddenly. A medical man who attended him remarking that he was suffering from diarrhoea and the effects of drinking bad whisky.

Alas, before the hearse arrived a party of officials from the local Coroner's office paid a visit and announced to the mourners that the funeral was cancelled and that the body was required for a post-mortem examination. This action had been instigated by the deceased man's brother, Patrick Higgins, who had been alarmed at the swiftness of his decline. The death, plus the rumours that abounded regarding his brother's wife and her sister, had led him to seek medical advice. Over the previous four years a number of deaths had occurred within the family and Patrick was determined to have the matter investigated.

The post-mortem examination confirmed his fears when it was announced that Thomas Higgins had died from arsenic poisoning. Both sisters had attended Thomas during his illness, and those present had noticed that when Catherine Flanagan gave him drink the man had suffered great pain.

Criminal investigations were at once proceeded with and it transpired that since 1880, when the sisters occupied a house in Skirving Street, a number of suspicious deaths had occurred. At that time the sisters had shared their home with five other people. These being Thomas Higgins – the future husband of Margaret, his young daughter Mary; a dock labourer Patrick Jennings, his teenage daughter Margaret; and John Flanagan, the son of Catherine Flanagan.

John Flanagan had died in December 1880, Mary Higgins in

Catherine Flanagan (top) and Margaret Higgins were hanged together for their ghastly crimes

November 1882, and Margaret Jennings in January 1883, and after each death the sisters had acted in haste to cash their life insurance policies. In each case death had followed a period of sickness when the sisters had played out the role of devoted nurses.

The belief was that all three young lives had been taken purely to obtain the financial benefits derived from cashing in the policies. This motive for murder took on greater reliability when it was learnt that on the life of Thomas Higgins, the sisters had taken out five policies. On the day of his death they had been paid £12.9s.6d by the British Workmen Insurance Company and £7.17s.6d from the Scottish Legal Life Assurance Society. The other Societies had not been so prompt in paying out and when news of the poisoning spread the likelihood of them doing so vanished. In all, the sisters had hoped to scoop £100 from the death of Thomas Higgins and the sum would have been £50 higher had not one insurance company insisted on a medical prior to issue of the policy. On the day of the intended medical, Thomas had apparently been drunk and the doctor had refused to carry out the examination. The awareness of these policies had heightened his brother Patrick's belief that the sisters had conspired to kill Thomas Higgins.

The suspicions of the police were also increased when Catherine Flanagan disappeared for over a week after the announcement of the forthcoming post-mortem. After spending some nights with friends and others in a lodging house in Mount Vernon, she was apprehended at the Station Hotel, Wellington Road, in the Wavertree district of Liverpool. A large crowd gathered to see her arrested and taken to the police station. In consequence of the public feeling that was building up against her, shouts of 'Poisoner' and 'Murderer' were hurled in her direction.

The two sisters stood on trial at Liverpool Assizes in the middle of February 1884, and the whole proceedings took just one day. Although the other indictments were listed the prosecution elected to proceed only with the murder of Thomas Higgins.

In their defence it was said that although the prosecution had proved that the women might have poisoned the man, it had not been proved that they were the only ones who could have done it. Surely, the Defence Counsel argued, it was only natural being sisters, that they should be present at the sick bed of one of their husband's.

The jury spent less than an hour to return a Guilty verdict and Mr Justice Butt then passed sentence of death on them both. The execution of the sisters took place on the first Monday in March 1884, at Kirkdale Gaol. The pair being hanged at eight o'clock in the morning by Bartholomew Binns and his assistant Samuel Heath.

Flanagan, though ghastly pale, required little assistance to reach the scaffold and showed no sign of nervousness. Higgins, on the other hand, seemed to have great difficulty in bearing up under the ordeal, and was supported up the steps by Heath and a female warder.

Having fixed the rope round the necks of the culprits, so that the knots came under the ear, the two executioners simultaneously touched the levers, the drop fell, and the women died instantaneously.

Chapter 23

A Joyful Journey turns to Grief

On Wednesday, September the 15th, 1830 the opening of the Liverpool and Manchester Railway took place. The occasion was a significant one and aroused great interest in both places joined together by 30 miles of dual track. A vast amount of capital had been expended on the project and final estimates reckoned that £800,000 (equivalent to upwards of £25 million pounds in today's money) had been spent to provide stations, machinery, waggons, and all the other requirements necessary.

The procession left Liverpool at exactly twenty minutes before eleven o'clock and was drawn by eight locomotive engines. The leading engine was the Northumbrian which carried the directors of the railway, and numerous distinguished visitors, including the Duke of Wellington. The other engines were the Phoenix, North Star, Rocket, Dart, Comet, Arrow and Meteor, all of which carried visitors and proprietors of the new enterprise.

On emerging from the small tunnel at Liverpool, The Northumbrian took the south, or right-hand line of railway, while the other seven proceeded along the north or left-hand line. The Northumbrian drew three carriages, the first containing the band, the second the Duke of Wellington and other persons of distinction, and the third the directors of the railway.

The carriage in which the Duke of Wellington and his friends travelled was truly magnificent. The floor was thirty two feet long by eight feet wide and was supported upon eight large iron wheels. The sides were beautifully ornamented with superb Grecian scrolls and gilded balustrades, supporting a handrail. A grand canopy, twenty four feet long was placed aloft upon gilded pillars and was designed so that it could be lowered to pass through a tunnel.

The other seven engines travelling on the adjacent line pulled either three, four or five carriages each and, in all, close to 800 passengers were on the first historical official journey.

The procession did not proceed at a particularly rapid pace – not more than 15 or 16 miles an hour. In the course of the journey the

Northumbrian accelerated or retarded its speed occasionally, to give the Duke of Wellington an opportunity of inspecting the most remarkable parts of the work.

On arrival at Parkside, the carriages stopped to take on a supply of water. Before starting from Liverpool the company were particularly requested not to leave the carriages and the same caution was repeated in the printed directions describing the order of the procession.

Notwithstanding this regulation, however, a number of gentlemen alighted from the Duke of Wellington's carriage as soon as it stopped at Parkside. Among those who alighted were two Members of Parliament, William Holmes and William Huskisson. At the moment they descended onto the track, three of the engines on the adjacent line, the Phoenix, the North Star and the Rocket, had passed on towards Manchester, and the other four, the Dart, Comet, Arrow and Meteor, were rapidly approaching.

William Huskisson, MP for Liverpool 1823-30, was to have a tragic end

Mr Huskisson and Mr Holmes were standing in the road between the two lines of railway, which were about four feet apart, just sufficient space for a person to stand while two engines passed each other. Unluckily, however, Mr Huskisson imagined that there was not enough room and when he saw the Dart approaching he made an attempt to get into the Duke of Wellington's carriage.

When *The Northumbrian* stopped at Parkside Station, the Liverpool MP descended onto the track with fatal consequences (19th century engraving)

With this view he laid hold of the door of the carriage and pulled it open with such force that he lost his balance and fell backwards across the rails of the other line.

The driver of the Dart immediately stopped it, but before this was completely effected, both wheels of the engine and one of those of the leading carriage had passed over the right leg of the unfortunate gentleman, who was placed across the rail, his head and body being under the engine.

A number of dignitaries immediately left the Duke of Wellington's carriage to tend to the injured Member of Parliament's needs. As he was raised from the ground he looked at those who aided him and said, "I have met my death – God forgive me".

He was at once placed aboard the Northumbrian engine, which was detached from its carriages, and sent forward with the greatest possible speed to Eccles, where two medical gentlemen, who were also aboard, hoped to be able to obtain surgical instruments.

On the arrival at Eccles, Mr Huskisson was conveyed to the local vicar's home, and the engine proceeded to Manchester to enlist further medical aid.

In Manchester the desire to witness the arrival and procession of the carriages pervaded all classes; and the day was generally observed as a holiday, from eleven o'clock business had almost entirely been suspended. From an early hour in the forenoon the banks of the railway were crowded with thousands of anxious spectators. Spacious stands erected at various points on the line were all fully occupied and the roofs of house and warehouses were vantage points for many.

The morning had continued fine from day break until about half-past twelve o'clock, when a rather severe thunderstorm passed over the town, accompanied with several heavy showers of rain. About five minutes past one o'clock, while the storm was still at its height, the approach of an engine was perceived along the railway and the Northumbrian immediately arrived in front of the warehouses.

To the surprise of everyone no carriages were attached to it and the only individuals in the tender, besides the fireman, were the Earl of Witton and Mr Stephenson, the engineer. On their alighting from the engine, it was immediately ascertained that a frightful accident had befallen Mr Huskisson, in the neighbourhood of Newton, and inquiry was instantly made for such medical gentlemen as might be present.

Fortunately three local surgeons were at hand, and after one of them had gathered his surgical instruments, the Northumbrian instantly set off on her return towards Eccles.

An impromptu consultation was held amongst the railways directors to decide what course to be adopted under the melancholy circumstances. It was finally agreed to proceed with the ceremony of opening the railway, to prevent, in some degree, the alarm and disappointment to the vast multitudes who thronged the Manchester end of the railway line.

The carriages of the Duke of Wellington and the Directors were consequently attached to the Phoenix engine, and in this manner they proceeded at a slow pace towards Eccles, where a stoppage took place while the Duke and his friends made enquiry respecting the condition of Mr Huskisson.

By this time the Northumbrian had arrived back from Manchester and was re-attached to the Duke's carriage and the whole were able to proceed in the order originally agreed upon. The Northumbrian eventually arriving in front of the warehouses at a quarter before three, with the other engines following a short time later.

On their arrival the company proceeded to the upper rooms of the warehouses to partake of a splendid lunch. The Duke of Wellington, however, declined in consequence of the accident to Mr Huskisson, and remained in his carriage where some light refreshments were handed to him. During the one and a half hours that the others dined, the Duke conversed with friends, and shook hands with the hundreds who thronged around him for that purpose. The Duke eventually took his departure at fifteen minutes past four, but the rest of the procession did not set off for some time afterwards.

Mr Huskisson, when taken into the house at Eccles, had been placed upon a couch in the drawing room. A bed was put up in the room but so great was his agony that until death it was never found practicable to remove him from the couch. From the same cause no part of his clothes were removed, except his cravat and one of his boots. The leg of his trousers was slit open to allow inspection of his wounds, and even his great coat remained around his shoulders until his hour of death. That came at nine o'clock that evening, after he had made some additions to his Will and received the sacraments.

News of his accident and subsequent death was received with shock in Liverpool, where he had been Member of Parliament for a number of years. At the inquest a verdict of "Accidentally Killed" was recorded on the Liverpool representative who was in his 61st year.

Postscript: A regular service of six passenger trains each day was established and travellers were able to travel 'inter-city' in 1½ hours at a cost of five or three shillings. Within two years the number of stage-coaches between the two places had fallen from thirty to one per day, and by 1840 the line was carrying half a million passengers per year.

Railway companies were formed in various parts of the country and in 1838 the Stephenson line was linked to the London-Birmingham line. Within twenty years, George Stephenson's railway had become part of a national network and rail travel was the main form of transport in Great Britain. The railways had become the 'arteries of the Industrial Revolution'.

Chapter 24

Arsenic and the Hypochondriac

On the last day of July in 1889, extraordinary interest was created when 25-year-old Florence Elizabeth Maybrick appeared at the Liverpool Assizes before Mr Justice Stephen, accused of the murder of her husband, James Maybrick who was in his late forties. It was claimed that Mrs Maybrick had caused the death of her cotton broker husband by the administering of arsenic poison.

The court was filled from an early hour on the opening day and a wave of sensation passed through the court as the prisoner walked up the steps and into the dock. She was dressed in mourning and wore a veil, beneath which her features were distinctly visible. With her slight and well proportioned figure and her light brown and frizzed hair she displayed a very attractive appearance.

When confronted with the charge of murder she declared, in a low but firm voice, that she was not guilty of the crime.

Over the next fortnight the case was laid before the jury and the prosecution went to great lengths to ensure her conviction. Their version of the events had those gathered totally absorbed in the proceedings.

They began by stating that Mr Maybrick had been a cotton broker in Liverpool with connections in America and, that on a visit to that country, he had met his future wife. The couple had married in July 1881, and three years later they had settled permanently in Liverpool. From their marriage they had two children, a boy who was seven and a girl who was three when their father died. The family had resided at Battlecrease House, Aigburth, where they kept up an establishment of some magnitude, having several servants to attend to their needs.

Then with the aid of various witnesses, the prosecution presented their version of the events that led to Mr Maybrick's demise. They started by showing that, according to his friends, James Maybrick was a strong and healthy man prior to his final year, although he had developed a habit of complaining about his liver and his nerves. In fact, over the previous eight years he had consulted Dr Hooper of Rodney Street, Liverpool and complained of numbness of the limbs,

Cotton broker James Maybrick was described as a hypochondriac

and the fear that it might produce paralysis. To calm his patient's fears the doctor had from time to time prescribed nerve tonics, but generally he had viewed Mr Maybrick as a hypochondriac, a view shared by his brothers and others who knew him.

It was revealed that in the middle of March 1889, Mrs Maybrick had visited London, telling her husband that she was going to the capital city to tend to an ailing aunt who was set to undergo an operation at the hands of a leading surgeon. Her visit however, was not for the purpose she claimed, because her days and nights away were spent in a private hotel in Cavendish Square, in the company of another Liverpool cotton broker, Alfred Brierley, the couple posing as man and wife.

On the 28th of March she had returned to Battlecrease House and the following day she accompanied her husband to the races to see the Grand National. Upon their return home the couple quarrelled and the day after Mrs Maybrick visited a lady friend, telling her that she had been struck by her husband and intended to get a separation.

As a result of their conversation, the two women visited Dr Hooper and he promptly visited Battlecrease House in his role as the family physician, and was successful in effecting a reconciliation between the Maybricks.

Two weeks later James Maybrick had visited his brother Michael in London and whilst there complained of feeling unwell. He was seen by his brother's physician who examined him, told him there was nothing organically wrong and treated him for dyspepsia. He had complained of numbness and pains in the head and although numbness was a symptom of arsenic poisoning, it was also a common symptom of numerous disorders and therefore not likely to cause any suspicion.

Sometime during the following week Mrs Maybrick had visited a neighbouring chemist and bought a dozen flypapers, each of which contained 2½ grains of arsenic. A housemaid later discovered the flypapers soaking in a basin of water in Mrs Maybrick's dressing room.

On the 20th of April Mr Maybrick returned home, but before he did so he once more visited the London physician who made up a prescription for him. As soon as he arrived back in Liverpool he went to a local chemist and had another bottle of the same medicine made up. The medicine from London was kept at his Liverpool office and the other bottle was taken home. After Mr Maybrick's death the two mixtures were analysed and the examination showed that the bottle taken home contained arsenic.

Great emphasis was placed on the deadly nature of the poison and experts related how two grains of arsenic taken at once would be enough to destroy life in twelve hours, the symptoms being excessive vomiting, purging and burning pains in the throat and stomach. The same symptoms being produced by smaller doses repeated often. Moreover, it was stated, arsenic rapidly passed through the system and despite its peculiarly dangerous qualities, in cases of death from its use little trace of it was ever found.

On the 27th of April Mr Maybrick made plans to visit Wirral races but prior to his departure he was seized by pain. He did however recover sufficiently to go on the outing, but the next morning and again at night he was in agony. A local practitioner was called to see him, and the following morning when he felt much improved the doctor prescribed a dietary mixture for him.

On that same day Mrs Maybrick visited another chemist's shop and obtained two dozen more flypapers. The prosecution stressed the fact that as her husband was recovering the woman was once again purchasing the arsenic contaminated flypaper.

Over the next three days Mr Maybrick busied himself at his Liverpool office and each lunch time he partook of the dietary mixture prescribed by the local doctor and made up by his wife. On the third evening when he returned home, he complained of being ill again and the following morning he was visited by the doctor. Throughout the day Mr Maybrick remained unwell and at midnight the doctor was again called out to attend a patient complaining of sickness and pains in the nerves. The next day he was very sick again and Mrs Maybrick was directed to place damp handkerchiefs to his mouth to relieve his thirst.

By the Sunday Mr Maybrick's condition had worsened and he remained in bed all day suffering from severe pain in his throat. Neither the medicine previously prescribed for him, nor another mixture, appeared to relieve his pain. In fact he began to complain to those who nursed him that the medicines given to him by his wife always made him sick.

It was felt that a trained nurse should be sent for and on the following Wednesday afternoon, a member of the Nurses Institution arrived. She administered to him some medicine handed to her by Mrs Maybrick and the nurse seemed confident that her patient would recover.

Later that day Mrs Maybrick gave the nurse a letter to post, which she opened and, having read it, gave it to Edwin Maybrick, the sick man's brother. The letter was addressed to Mr Brierley and appeared to be in answer to one received from him a couple of day's previously.

The jury was to hear the contents of both letters and in his, Mr Brierley had spoken about making a trip to the Mediterranean unless Mrs Maybrick desired him to stay. He also spoke of it not being safe for them to meet until the autumn. In her reply Mrs Maybrick had referred to her husband saying, "Since my return I have been nursing him day and night. He is sick unto death. The doctors held a consultation yesterday, and now all depends on how long his strength will hold out. I cannot answer your letter fully today, my darling, but relieve your mind of all fear of discovery, now and in future".

The letter then went on to explain that her husband had no suspicion of what had transpired in London, and urged Mr Brierley not to leave England until she had seen him again.

The jury were told that up until the Thursday, which was the 11th of May, the doctors attributed the illness to acute dyspepsia, but on that evening it was concluded that Mr Maybrick was suffering from irritant poisoning.

On the same evening the nurse in attendance opened a fresh bottle of Valentine's meat extract and a few minutes later she observed Mrs Maybrick taking the bottle in a stealthy manner into her dressing room. Within a couple of minutes she returned the bottle and placed it in the same way on the table. Her actions aroused the nurse's suspicions and the next morning she handed it to one of Mr May-brick's brothers. A subsequent analysis of the contents was to show that the meat extract contained half a drachm of arsenic.

Within another twenty four hours the condition of Mr Maybrick was hopeless and as the day ended so did the life of the Liverpool cotton broker.

After the death the house was searched and arsenic was found in various places and bottles. In Mrs Maybrick's dressing gown was discovered a handkerchief saturated with arsenic.

The post-mortem on the deceased showed the organs to be healthy, but there were traces of arsenic in the bowels, kidneys and liver. The medical verdict, the jury were informed, was that death was due to arsenic poison, given in repeated doses.

After the prosecution's damning evidence had been presented, the defence Counsel set about rescuing the situation. As they delivered their response it was claimed that Mr Maybrick was always dosing himself, and had told friends that he regularly took arsenic as an aphrodisiac. The jury were also told that in 1887 Mrs Maybrick had learned that her husband was keeping a mistress. Around the same time the husband had run into financial problems and had forced his wife to reduce her spending.

The defence suggested that Maybrick died a natural death and that the poison found in his body was the result of hypochondriac dosing. As to the flypapers purchased by Mrs Maybrick it was claimed that she used them to make an arsenical cosmetic preparation.

When all the evidence and arguments had ended, Mr Justice Stephens summed up heavily against the unfaithful wife. On the final day of the trial Mrs Maybrick entered the dock a little apprehensively and once again she had to face the glare of a crowded court. The jury retired to consider their verdict shortly before three o'clock in the afternoon.

The public opinion of the likely verdict was divided and one group of ladies were so confident that Mrs Maybrick would be acquitted that they had in readiness a magnificent bouquet. When it was announced within the hour that the jury was returning, many thought it was a favourable sign for an acquittal. The silence and tension of the moment was most impressive. After being asked to deliver their verdict, the foreman of the jury announced in a low voice, "Guilty".

At the moment of the verdict Mrs Maybrick dropped her head down on one hand, resting it almost on one knee, and sat in that attitude for almost fifteen seconds amidst the profoundest silence.

When asked if she had anything to say why sentence of death should not be passed, she rose to her feet and in a firm voice said that whatever her guilt with regard to Mr Brierley, she was not guilty of the crime, adding that evidence had been withheld which, if the jury knew it, their opinion might have been different.

The Judge then assumed the black cap and, in a tone which showed he was deeply affected, informed Mrs Maybrick that she would be hung by the neck until dead. As he spoke the dreaded words the woman was seen to tremble and as his Lordship completed his speech with the words, "May the Lord have mercy upon your soul", she bowed her head in reverence and clasped her hands in front of her. She then left the dock walking down the steps with great firmness with a female warder on either side.

Mr Justice Stephens pronounced a sentence of death

As the jury were about to be discharged loud hisses were heard throughout the court and when the verdict became known to the great multitude outside the St. George's Hall, there were loud groans and hooting. Upon his departure, His Lordship Mr Justice Stephens found his carriage surrounded by a large crowd and they yelled and hooted as the coach was driven rapidly away.

Shortly before six o'clock that evening a crowd of several hundred persons assembled at the south side of St. George's Hall to see the departure of Mrs Maybrick in the prison van bound for Walton gaol. The crowd of people were obviously in sympathy with Mrs Maybrick and as the black and melancholy vehicle drove through the streets to Walton, it was cheered to the echo by thousand of bystanders. Men and women ran after it and the driver had to whip his horses to get away from the crowds.

Her execution was set to take place three weeks later at Walton Gaol but three days before the dreaded hour a messenger arrived at the prison with an Order from the Home Secretary, commuting the sentence to one of life imprisonment.

In all she served fifteen years in prison with the first nine months being in solitary confinement. Her elegant gowns had been replaced by the dowdy prison dress and her main diet had become one of bread and porridge.

Many campaigners continually petitioned for her release and eventually in January 1904, she regained her freedom. With an escort provided by the American ambassador, the girl from Alabama crossed to France to visit her aged mother.

Florence Elizabeth Maybrick – there was great sympathy for her plight

She then returned to America where she enjoyed celebrity status giving interviews and writing a book, "My lost fifteen years". After a while she disappeared from the headlines and settled down in a village called South Kent in Connecticut. She chose a lonely existence surrounded by dozens of cats whom she had great affection for. Her death occurred in October 1941, and her last years were said to have been lived in neglect and squalor.

Chapter 25

Triple Tragedy at The Barracks

The town and neighbourhood of Burnley, was, on the evening of Sunday November 14th, 1841, thrown into a state of great excitement and confusion by news of a shocking tragedy at the local barracks. The barracks at Burnley, erected in 1821, covered a large area and generally was occupied by both cavalry and infantry.

At the time stationed there were troops of the Second Dragoon Guards in the cavalry part of the barracks, and the infantry section was tenanted by two companies of the 60th Rifles, under the command of Major Cockburn. The terrible incidents occurred within the mess house, a detached building in the barrack yard.

The officers, as was their custom, dined in the mess room at seven o'clock that evening. An hour later Lieutenant O'Grady excused himself from the gathering of officers, a much earlier time than he generally retired after dinner.

Some thirty minutes later, with Major Cockburn and several other officers still in the room, they were astounded by the re-appearance of Lt. O'Grady. Rushing into the room he staggered towards the hearth, exclaiming – "Major Cockburn – Morris has murdered me!". He then fell upon the hearth rug apparently exhausted from the loss of blood. His clothes were by this time drenched in blood from a large wound on his left side.

As the officers crowded around him, loud screams were heard from the direction of the unfortunate man's apartment and Major Cockburn rushed from the room to ascertain the cause of this fresh alarm. On entering the lobby he saw lying, not far from Lt. O'Grady's room, Isabella Hadden, a servant girl. Major Cockburn's attention was then drawn towards Robert Morris, a private in the regiment, who was at the far end of the lobby, brandishing a large carving knife and apparently about to make his exit from the building.

Major Cockburn, with a view of intercepting the flight of the murderer, turned round and ran out of the front entrance of the mess house and round the front of the building towards the back door of the lobby. As he ran, he called, "Order the Guard out; and sentry, stop everybody that passes!". Having reached the back door, Major Cockburn entered the building once again and there he found Morris, stretched on his back, apparently dead from self inflicted wounds. The knife which had been used for the fearful deeds was lying on the ground a short distance from his feet.

For a short while pandemonium reigned in the building and amongst those whose shrieks and cries filled the air were those of the injured girl's mother, herself a mess room attendant. She had been a witness to the attack on Lt. O'Grady and within a minute heard of her daughter's terrible ordeal.

Lt. O'Grady was at once attended by a surgeon of the regiment and as he was comforted in his dying condition he told those gathered around him, "Oh! I have long expected this from that villain". With great care he was placed upon a table and conveyed to his own room where he was laid upon a bed. He had lost a great deal of blood and in his weak condition he lingered until ten-thirty on the Monday morning, at which time he expired.

When the poor girl was raised from the ground it was found she was bleeding profusely from several wounds inflicted below her shoulder on the left side. She was conveyed to the room of her mother, where a medical man shortly attended her. Much pain was endured by her and she only survived until eleven o'clock that Sunday night.

Robert Morris was instantly raised and carried to his room and he expired within a couple of minutes. He had apparently stabbed himself with such desperation as to inflict two or three mortal wounds. The weapon he had used was about a foot in length – being an old carver, much ground and so thin that the back had almost as sharp an edge as the true edge; the point too, was very sharp. The force with which the knife had been used was evident from the blade being quite bent and the point being almost turned, as if it had come into contact with some hard substance, such as bone.

All were anxious to know the cause of this three-fold tragedy and it appeared that it had been activated by jealousy. There had been considerable intimacy between William Sharman O'Grady and the girl and Morris was jealous of this, and desirous that she should marry him, strangely enough, for he was aware that she was already married.

On Sunday afternoon Morris and the girl, who was 20 years old and had married some years before, had taken a walk towards the town. During the walk Morris was said to have reproached her about the attention she gave to the officer and to have threatened that he would be the death of them both. On their return to the barracks, Morris waited at dinner as usual, but when asked by the mess-woman, the mother of the deceased girl, to come to supper as he had been accustomed to do, he replied "I'll have no supper", and walked out of the room.

On quitting the mess room Lt. O'Grady had gone to his own apartment, where the girl was waiting for him. When she revealed the threats made by Morris, the officer immediately went to the mess waiters' pantry, to demand that Morris should deliver up his sword and rifle.

As soon as the lieutenant made known to the private why he sought him, the latter snatching up the carving knife commenced his bloody work. After stabbing Lt. O'Grady, Morris rushed past the wounded officer to his apartment, where he suspected the girl to be. Aroused by the action in the adjoining room, the girl was about to make her escape when she was confronted at the door by Morris. He immediately lunged the murder weapon into her, stabbing her repeatedly in the side and back. A large splash of blood on the wall near the door being testimony to his terrible action.

Soon details began to emerge of the three deceased persons. Robert Morris, in his mid-twenties, was of Scottish origin, being a native of Aberdeen and had spent eleven years in the regiment. He was considered a good, steady, trustworthy man and nothing had been alleged against him, except some former quarrels with the girl, to whom he appeared devoutly attached. It was said that on one occasion the lieutenant had ordered him into confinement for some neglect of duty, or act of insubordination.

Isabella Hadden, as she was generally called, was said to have long been of indifferent character. When only sixteen years old she had married a man named Patrick Terrett, a private in the 97th regiment, who was at the time stationed at the Burnley barracks. She had for four years been living separate from her husband, who was in Malta with this regiment. She was employed by her mother as a kitchen assistant. She had an infant daughter of two years age who was in the care of a nurse in the neighbourhood of Burnley.

The unfortunate officer was from an illustrious Irish military family, being a nephew of the late Lord Chief Baron of the Irish Exchequer. His mother was said to reside in Dublin and, according to reports, it was the second time she was doomed to mourn over the premature death of a son; a brother of the deceased having been shot

THE BURNLEY MURDER

You young men and maidens one moment attend
Unto a true story as ever was penned,
These lines are concerning a sad tragedy,
Occasioned and prompted by cursed jealousy.

On November the fourteenth, eighteen hundred and forty-one,
In the Barracks, near Burnley, this sad deed was done,
By one Robert Morris, a soldier we hear,
In the 60th Rifles, which was stationed there.

There was a young girl in the mess house we find,
On whom this young soldier had fixed his mind;
But there was another her favour had won,
Young Lieutenant Grady, a nobleman's son.

"My dear Isabella," young Morris did cry,
"If thus you do slight me, I'm sure I shall die,
So now truly promise you will be my wife,
Or else I'm determined to take your sweet life."

Isabella and Grady in company were,
When Morris before them did sudden appear,
"Inconstant woman," enraged he did cry,
"If we can't live together-together we must die".

Then a large butcher's knife young Morris he drew,
And Lieutenant Grady he stabbed through and through,
Who unto the Major did stagger away,
Crying "Help, private Morris has murdered me."

Then towards Isabella the maniac did turn
With love, rage, and hatred his bosom did burn,
The Murderous knife he plunged into her side,
"Have mercy, dear Morris, have mercy," she cried.

She begged for mercy, but it was all in vain,
He cut and he stabbed her again and again;
Her blood ran in streams, her bright eyes lost their fire,
"Oh Morris," she cried, and did shortly expire.

Meantime the alarm in the Barracks was made,
Both officers and men ran to offer their aid,
While the murderer appeared with his deed satisfied,
Stabbed himself to the heart, and then instantly died.

Thus fell those three victims in their youth and bloom,
Both murderer and murdered are now in the tomb;
Young people beware of accursed jealousy,
For that was the cause of this sad tragedy.

A verse recorded the tragic story

in a duel some years previously, an affair which at the time caused considerable sensation in Dublin. He was said to be in his 30th year and had been with the 60th Rifles since 1834. Those who knew him described him as hot headed and at times intemperate, but he was generally much liked by the soldiers of the regiment.

On the following Wednesday an Inquest was held into the deaths of the three ill-fated individuals. After viewing the bodies the jury were subjected to the testimony of various witnesses who outlined the events of the fateful Sunday evening.

After deliberating for about twenty minutes, at the end of an eight hour hearing, the jury came to the following verdict; That William Sharman O'Grady and Isabella Terrett (nee Hadden) had been murdered by Robert Morris; and that the said Robert Morris, in destroying himself, had been guilty of 'felo-de-se'.

Chapter 26

A Shocking Street Tragedy

Shortly after five o'clock on the afternoon of the 12th of June 1895, the district of Penny Street, Blackburn, a densely populated neighbourhood, was thrown into the wildest state of excitement when it became known that a terrible tragedy had occurred in Starkie Street.

The individuals at the centre of the deed were George Bradley, aged 39, a native of Blackburn and his paramour Margaret Walmsley, some ten years his junior. The tragedy took only a few seconds to perpetrate and was witnessed by a local youth.

Bradley and the woman were noticed near the entrance to the corn mill of Mr Noblett in Starkie Street and they appeared to be quarrelling. In a moment the woman was seen to run across the street carrying a baby in her arms. Bradley immediately produced a revolver and pointing it in the direction of Margaret Walmsley, fired. She at once fell on to the footpath and the child fell out of her arms. A second shot was then fired at the woman who, quickly regaining her feet, ran in the direction of Penny Street and, after running some distance, fell insensible.

At the first alarm the neighbours were brought to their doors and three or four of them saw Bradley fire the second shot at his paramour. Bradley was standing in the roadway and a man sent a stone at him in the hope of dispossessing him of the revolver, as he was by now presenting the firearm at himself. Bradley quickly covered the man with his revolver and the fellow beat a hasty retreat.

Then, without a moment's hesitation, Bradley placed the revolver to his face and, to the horror of the bystanders, discharged the weapon. He slumped to the ground and before the spectators realised what was happening, Bradley lay dead before them.

Crowds were quickly attracted to the spot and the throng struggled to get a glimpse of the lifeless body. The face presented a shocking sight, blood having streamed from a wound underneath his left eye, and from a second one just above the left ear. A local doctor was soon on the scene and after examining the body he arranged for it to be conveyed to the mortuary at the Central Police Station.

Fortunately, Margaret Walmsley was not as badly injured as at first thought. She was immediately taken to the Infirmary and treated for a gunshot wound and injuries to her head, which were obtained when she fell in the street. By the following morning she was said to be well on the way to recovery.

At once investigations began to piece together the reason for the terrible tragedy. Regarding Bradley, it was said he started his working life in a boiler works in Blackburn and that afterwards he became a clogger. He then commenced to travelling the country as a grinder, paying occasional visits to Blackburn.

About 1890 when on one of his trips home he met Margaret Walmsley and within a few months they were living together as man and wife. As their relationship developed the couple had three children, the eldest died, the second was a bright boy and the third, a girl, was just four months old at the time of the incident.

Bradley appeared to have settled down and for a good while ran a brokers shop in Larkhill, which eventually he removed to Penny Street. It was said that the pair did not live happily together; that Bradley took all the money they got from the shop, and that he only allowed her a miserable pittance for house-keeping purposes. This treatment by Bradley led to his being summoned before the Magistrates and through this Margaret Walmsley obtained two Orders of 3s.6p per week against Bradley for the support of her children.

Bradley was none too pleased with his mistress's action and he gave her a sovereign and sent her off to her sister's for six weeks. When she returned to Blackburn a few days later Bradley had disposed of his business as a broker and sailed for America.

Margaret Walmsley then took up lodgings in Penny Street for about a month and later, with the help of friends, she was able to furnish a small terraced house in a nearby street. Settled in her new home she managed to earn a living for herself and the children by sewing.

Bradley, however, returned suddenly from America and hearing that Margaret Walmsley had been lodging in Penny Street, went to enquire of her whereabouts. During the few days, prior to the tragedy, he saw her a couple of times, although he did not find out she had taken a place of her own.

He tried to persuade her to go back to him, but she told him that her mind was made up, that she would not live with him again as he refused to marry her. She received a final message from him on the afternoon of the incident, and she met him in Starkie Street with the resultant tragic ending.

All the acquaintances spoke well of Margaret Walmsley and it was related that when she first arrived in Blackburn she earned her living by hawking. She was said to be of temperate habits and that following her example, Bradley himself had been teetotal for three years prior to their separation.

This shocking street tragedy perpetrated by the attempted murderer completely stunned the people of Blackburn, and it was apparent that Bradley's actions were premeditated. The revolver he possessed was a new one and it had been loaded in all six chambers, all of which had been discharged.

Chapter 27

When we Venture to Deceive

During the week before Christmas, in 1863 Luke Charles, a tall well built and fine looking man appeared at the South Lancashire Assizes, before Mr Justice Willes, accused of the murder of his wife Mary. Charles, who had been a police officer with the Bury constabulary, had been married to the deceased for nine years. They had been married in Ireland at a place called Colbridge in County Kildare, where the prisoner had at the time been in the Irish constabulary. Due the fact that the couple had been married without permission of the police authorities, they did not live together.

Later, he succeeded in joining the English police and in August 1862, his wife, who had remained in Ireland living with friends, joined him. Based in Bury, the constable obtained various lodgings for himself and his wife in that town, eventually living with a widow, Sarah Porrith, who resided at a place called 'Tenter's-Fold'.

Alas, their reunion was not a particularly happy one, with Charles, instead of being true to his wife, actually visiting and corresponding with another young woman, Ellen Ford, who was back in Ireland living at Emo, in Queen's County.

The crime Charles was accused of was said to have occurred in February 1863, his wife having disappeared on the 13th day of that month. On the day in question Charles and his wife had left their lodgings about five o'clock in the afternoon, telling Mrs Porrith that they were going to visit her sister, Julia Dunn, who lived in Clegg Court, Pendleton near Manchester. Mrs Charles did not return that night and when Mrs Porrith enquired as to her whereabouts, Luke Charles said she had gone to Ireland to see her mother. Later that evening he complained of feeling ill and did not go on duty for a week, being visited on one occasion by the police surgeon.

As the weeks passed by, Julia Dunn became worried about her sister's absence and began to quiz her brother-in-law. In March she had received a letter from Luke Charles saying her sister was away and a visit to Bury at the beginning of May heightened her fears. On that occasion Charles claimed Mary was in Ireland and Julia expressed disbelief, informing him that if he would not tell her where

Mary was, then perhaps he would be made to tell. To which he replied, "If I don't know they can't make me tell".

The weeks of doubt turned into months for Julia Dunn, with her brother-in-law continually claiming his wife was in Ireland. Eventually, in August, the matter came to a head after Luke Charles had been over to Ireland. When he returned Julia visited his lodgings in Bury, asking, "Have you brought Mary back with you?". His reply was a puzzling one, saying to her that her sister had requested that he did not tell her where she was.

Julia was finally convinced that something was amiss and determined to find out what, she went to the police station. She told of her sister's disappearance and the husband's strange behaviour. The police at once went through the files of unidentified deaths and came across details of the discovery of a body, on St. Valentine's Day of that year, in the Manchester, Bolton & Bury Canal at Pendleton. The description matched in many ways that of Mary Charles and Miss Dunn was taken to the Salford Workhouse, where the clothes and personnel effects of the woman were being kept.

When the body had been pulled out of the canal, a cloak (with a scarlet lining), a nightdress, a cap and some copper coins wrapped in paper had been discovered. These items, as well as Mary's wedding ring, convinced Julia that her sister was in fact the poor woman dragged out of the canal.

Permission to exhume the body was immediately applied for and investigations into a possible murder got underway. The subsequent examination of the body revealed few marks of violence and the possibility of an accident or suicide could not be ruled out.

Investigations led the authorities to believe that Luke Charles had committed murder and hence to his appearance in the dock. In court it was revealed that in August he had been back to Ireland in the company of Ellen Ford. She told how the pair of them had been intending to marry and of the fact that she had come over to England with him after his last visit, lodging firstly in Bury. Miss Ford had been completely oblivious of the fact that Luke Charles was a married man.

Various witnesses were called to build up the case against Luke Charles but throughout the trial he preserved the same calm, firm and cheerful demeanour.

When the Defence Counsel addressed the jury on his behalf, he spoke in some length, contending that the accused had not murdered his wife, but that she had gone away; and that the prisoner had then told one lie after another, until he had got himself into his present dilemma. He finished by saying, "Oh, what a tangled web we weave, when first we venture to deceive".

Mr Justice Willes told the jury that the facts of the case must be consistent in their minds to find the prisoner guilty. It took the jury half an hour to record a verdict of 'Guilty' and his Lordship then put on the black cap and spoke as follows:- "Luke Charles, you have been convicted of the wilful murder of your wife by evidence which the jury, after patient consideration and with good reason, considered to be sufficient to establish your guilt. It is no part of the duty of this court to aggravate your position – the dreadful position in which you stand; but it is my duty to warn you that your days are numbered and that you must soon appear before your maker, and give to Him an account of all your actions. I exhort and charge you to spend the few days remaining of your life endeavouring to obtain the mercy which is promised to all who repent".

Sentence of death was then pronounced and the prisoner, upon hearing it, bowed his head. He then turned round and slowly descended the steps leading from the dock.

On the second Saturday of January 1864, a crowd of five or six thousand gathered outside Kirkdale Gaol to witness the public execution of the former policeman. Five minutes before noon the large iron doors leading to the drop were opened by a gaoler, whose appearance at once created great excitement amongst the crowd. At exactly mid-day the culprit stepped firmly beneath the fatal beam. He had his eyes closed, and never opened them during the rest of his life. He was accompanied on the scaffold by the Rev Gibson and Captain Gibbs, the governor of the gaol. The executioner, Calcraft, quickly put on the white cap and, having adjusted the noose and bound the culprits feet, he bade him farewell. In another second Luke Charles was despatched from this life. So sudden and so deep was the drop that the rebound was truly awful and the man appeared to have died instantaneously as he was not seen to move after falling.

After the execution Captain Gibbs was interviewed by the press and he said that when Luke Charles was asked as to his guilt or innocence, he had replied that he did not wish to say anything. The only visitors he had received whilst awaiting execution were his brother from Liverpool and Mrs Porrith, his former landlady.

Chapter 28

Rushing Headlong to Disaster

Towards the end of the nineteenth century, day trips to the seaside were a popular pastime amongst Lancashire folk and to this end the Church of St. Mary's at Wigan organised a visit for their catholic choir to Blackpool. The date of the excursion was Saturday, July 1st, 1893 and the choir caught a special train which had been put on to accommodate the increased traffic.

The train started from Stockport shortly after mid-day and its engine was under the control of two Stockport men, Cornelius Ridgeway an experienced driver aged 47, and William Henry Lowe, the fireman. After calling at the intervening stations the train stopped at Wigan where the members of the catholic choir climbed aboard. In all there were 50 or 60 passengers on the train which consisted of a powerful engine and tender, three carriages mostly third class, and a brake van.

Blackpool was reached without any problems and from mid afternoon the passengers enjoyed the delights of the seaside resort with its many attractions. Indeed, the party of visitors were given ample time to indulge themselves with the return trip scheduled for eleven o'clock that night.

That evening the train left Talbot Road, Blackpool on time and was soon making good speed, with one passenger being heard to tell his brother, "If we go at this rate we shall soon be back at Wigan".

Unfortunately, the train was fast approaching the notorious Poulton curve which had been created a few years earlier with the doubling of the main lines. Although the curve, which was strongly fenced, had accommodated up to a hundred special trains at the height of the season, there had been strong feeling in the public mind as to the dangers of such a sharp bend. In consequence the railway companies had stipulated that the speed of the trains around the curve must not exceed five miles per hour.

On this occasion the danger appeared to go unheeded and the train approached the curve at a considerable pace. The passengers from the church choir were singing and taking little notice as the carriages began to oscillate. Suddenly, at a point about 80 yards from the Poulton station and three-quarters way round the bend, the engine left the rails and leapt the steel guards.

The passengers were jolted and the cry, "We're off the line", was heard. Within seconds the carriages fell on their side, the lamps flew out and the passengers were pitched one over the other as the train was ripped to pieces, with the roof falling in and debris trapping many inside.

The engine, after leaving the metals, ran parallel with the lines for a few yards and then reeling sharply to the left, it struck a triangular bank of land in the fork where the Blackpool and Fleetwood lines converged. With great force the engine ploughed away a quantity of earth and demolished the petroleum store located there, which happily did not ignite, and then plunged straight across the lines. The engine dragged after it the three passenger carriages and, after rocking violently, it suddenly heeled over with the tender to the left, the fire flying from the box. The stoker leapt away and escaped with bruises, but the driver stuck to his charge and fell under the engine as she went over.

The notorious curve at Poulton, scene of the tragic accident.

The passenger carriages were all wrecked and partly telescoped, the body of one of the carriages being forced partly onto the engine. Another had swung against a coal waggon in the siding opposite and the third carriage was smashed into fragments, as was the brake van.

The accident, with its terrible consequences, occurred within a few seconds, and the crash could be heard at a long distance. The air was filled with shrieks and moans and piteous cries for help, the horror of the situation being intensified by the steam which was blowing off from the boiler. A few of the passengers found themselves pitched on to the metals and although slightly bruised they at once set to work to help those who were in the wreckage.

Some parts of the carriages were splintered to matchwood and many passengers were literally caged. Many had been cut by the shattered windows and others were pierced and scratched with the splinters of the timbers. The bodies of some were free, but their legs were wedged and they implored helpers to get them out.

The passengers in the first two carriages suffered the most severely, though fortunately, the first two compartments in the first carriage, which were first class, were empty.

Within a short time a large body of men were at the scene and railway, police and medical personnel toiled to extract the victims from the tangled mass. The injured were removed in haste and those who could not walk were carried on stretchers to either the Royal Hotel or the Railway and Station Hotel in nearby Poulton.

One poor woman was trying to help her husband who was trapped. Desperately she gripped his hand tightly as she called to him excitedly, but he made no reply. After great difficulty he was lifted out of the wreckage and found to be dead. His neck had been broken and his head terribly bruised. The woman was convulsed with grief and later it was revealed that he was 40-year-old James Marsh, the father of her five children and that they came from Wigan, being members of the catholic choir party.

Shortly after, James Healey a school boy from Wigan, who was another member of the choir party, was pulled from the debris. His skull had been fractured and his lifeless body was removed to the parlour of the Royal Hotel, where it was laid next to that of Marsh.

A powerful engine, cranes, waggons and equipment was sent from Preston and when the damaged engine was raised, the body of the driver was discovered at his post. There were only a few marks on

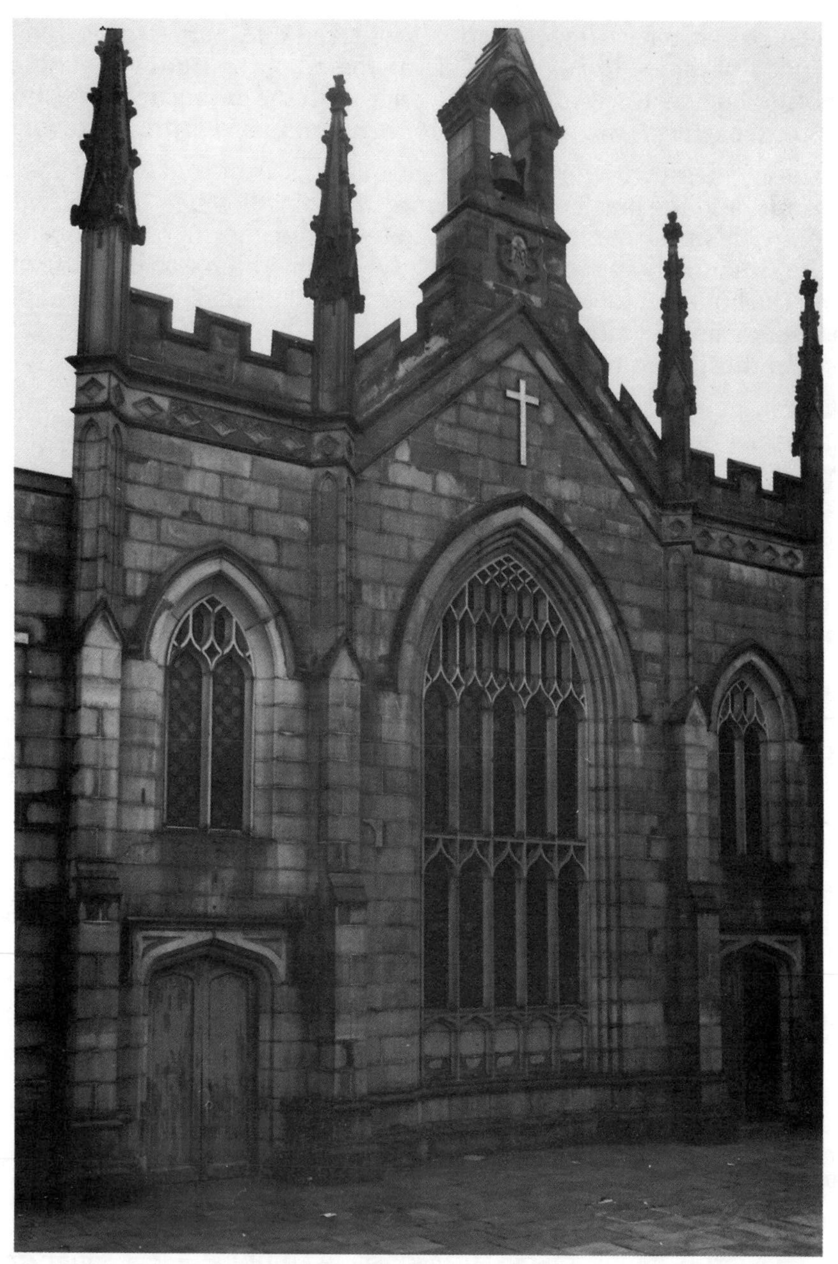

The choir from St. Mary's church at Wigan were treated to an ill-fated Blackpool excursion

his forehead, he was free from fractures and had evidently died from suffocation.

Over thirty passengers suffered injury, yet considering the nature of the accident it was regarded as miraculous that only three persons had lost their lives. In fact, most of the wounded had escaped with slight injuries and by day break plans were afoot to lay on a special train to ferry them back home.

The second carriage had been the most crowded and the list of casualties, with a few exceptions, was confined to members of St. Mary's catholic choir from Wigan. They had been sat close together and united in song after their exciting day at the seaside when overcome by the tragedy.

By midnight the injured and the dead had been got out and the task of clearing the line was undertaken. This was done in haste and by six o'clock on the Sunday morning it was complete.

When the official enquiry took place, Poulton station's notorious curve was condemned and the railway company was charged with culpable negligence. In consequence the Poulton station was closed and relocated higher up the Breck, much nearer to the village.

Postscript: It was later revealed that Cornelius Ridgeway, the engine driver killed in the accident, had been one of the three railway men concerned in the capture of the Netherby burglars who had been hung at Carlisle in 1886. On that occasion, Ridgeway had shown great courage in apprehending one of the three felons, fastening him to a signal post with a rope.

Chapter 29

Double Life led to The Gallows

Sometime in 1887, Joseph Mellor, a factory operative described by his acquaintances as a drunkard, set up home in Hollins Road, Oldham, with a woman who was a former street walker, herself partial to more than a sensible amount of drink. The couple seemed to survive successfully together and in August 1889, the pair were married. However, it did not seem to be a marriage made in heaven and within two years Mellor was courting another female, a Miss Sunderland.

His new found love was unaware of Mellor's marital ties and he continued the deception as their affair blossomed. By Christmas 1891, he had proposed to her and set the following Christmas as the date for their wedding.

By the summer of 1892, Mellor was finding it impossible to get on with a wife at home and another in prospect. It was then he determined to get rid of his lawful spouse and he set about the task in a deliberate and methodical manner.

From the end of August, Mellor was frequently with his intended bride and it was shortly after that suspicions were aroused. Once, when taxed about his wife, he had replied, "Don't mention Jenny; it's off with her. I'm going to be married shortly to a respectable young woman".

Eventually, on the 19th of October a woman neighbour, concerned about the absence of Mrs Mellor, went into the back yard of Mellor's home and climbed onto a chair to look through the kitchen window. She observed the kitchen flags torn up and a hole dug. At once she informed the police who, on entering the house, found the body of Mrs Mellor in the cellar. The deceased woman had been frightfully butchered. Her skull had been fractured from ear to ear and her throat cut right across with all the arteries being severed. Besides these horrendous injuries there were also no fewer than seven stab wounds in her chest.

The police immediately went to Melrose Mill where Mellor was employed and when arrested he practically admitted his crime. The police officer said, "I suppose you know what I've come for", and Mellor replied, "Yes, it's all right". Then turning to the cashier he said, "Pay me up, Robert, I shall never come back here again".

After his arrest Mellor seemed keen to have Miss Sunderland implicated in the crime and on the 9th of November, from his prison cell in Strangeways, he wrote the following note to the authorities.

"Dear Sir, Miss Sunderland knowed as much as me about the Hollins Road crime. She has been there four times after eleven at night since the Wakes. I will tell you more after my trial. Then I will tell you all, Joseph Mellor.

In fact during the subsequent trial at Manchester Assizes, Mellor made gross charges against a number of people, all of which were entirely disproved, including those against Miss Sunderland.

When found guilty he behaved with the utmost unconcern. Throughout the trial he betrayed no emotion and when the Judge asked him if he had anything to say as to why sentence of death should not be passed upon him, he at once started to speak in a voice which was heard throughout the court. It was a frenzied speech of two or three minutes and he asserted vehemently that three quarters of the evidence brought against him were lies, and he said if he had had money at his back he could have disproved it. He made charges of falsehood against specific witnesses, and twice said, "I would not care if I was being hanged this minute".

When he stopped in his speech, the Judge asked him, "Have you anything more to say?" to which the prisoner replied in a savage tone, "I've no more to say; get on wi' it". Sentence was then passed and as Mellor was removed he shouted, "It's all over wi' me now".

The date of execution for the 33-year-old murderer was fixed for Tuesday, December 20th 1892. The afternoon before, he was visited by his father. The conversation between the two touched on a few family matters, but the subject of the crime was avoided by the prisoner. When asked if he had any further statement to make, he remarked that he had said all he was going to say.

Several hundred persons gathered outside Strangeways Prison, Manchester to await the hoisting of the black flag, but there was no demonstration of any kind. The reporters were later informed by the Governor of the Gaol that James Billington had been the executioner, and that a drop of 7 feet was allowed. It was reported that Mellor made no statement of any kind and that there were no unusual features about the execution.

Chapter 30

Tell My Wife, I Die Happy

In 1889, there was a business called Gordon Furnishing Company, which traded in Manchester (opposite the Assizes Court building), with branches in Bury, Burnley and other towns. The management of the Bury shop was in the hands of a respectably connected young married man, called William Dukes. For sometime he discharged his duties satisfactorily but he eventually got drinking and acquired other loose habits, which led to the business being neglected.

As a result, on the last Wednesday in September 1889, George Gordon, of Jewish descent and one of the partners in the family run business, was sent over from Manchester to Bury to investigate matters. During his visit he was seen at the Bury shop by several persons employed there, but as the day progressed each were sent away by Dukes on one pretext or another, and the two men were left alone in the premises.

That same night Dukes despatched a telegram to Manchester in Gordon's name, purporting to inform the young man's father that he had gone on to the Burnley shop. When, however, George Gordon did not make his appearance at home, inquiries were instituted and it was found that he had not been to the Burnley shop at all.

His father, Simeon Gordon, and a brother at once became alarmed and, going over to Bury, they obtained the assistance of the police in order to search the business premises. Their initial search uncovered nothing except that several flags in the cellar appeared as though they had been loosened. Later, though, the father had his attention drawn to a wardrobe which was at the back of the store room. He immediately asked for it to be opened, but Dukes told him it was sold and was due to be sent to Rochdale. When pressed to open it he acted strangely and claimed that the key was not at hand. The father insisted on having the wardrobe broken open and when the door was forced a terrible discovery was made.

Inside the wardrobe lay the body of George Gordon. It had been doubled up, so as to crowd it into the wardrobe's recess. The head was shockingly battered, the face bruised, the throat cut and one of the eyes almost forced out.

Duke's was immediately taken into custody and when questioned he said, "I'll tell you all about it", but he offered no further explanation until his trial took place.

The discovery of the body led to a thorough search of the premises and on the floor were found marks of blood which had been covered with whitening and varnished in an attempt to conceal them. Also found were a hammer and a chisel, both of which had blood stains upon them.

The trial of William Dukes, aged 27, for the murder of George Gordon at Bury, took place at Manchester Assizes at the beginning of December. The crowded state of the court demonstrated the extra-ordinary amount of public interest. Mr Justice Charles presided and Dukes, a man of short stature and stout build, appeared in the dock in a loose light coloured coat, dark vest and dark trousers. He had a careworn appearance and seemed somewhat unconcerned as the proceedings progressed.

Medical experts were called to describe the state of the victim's body and it was revealed that the skull had been fractured in several places. In their opinion the fractures had been caused by the man being struck from behind, and had most probably been caused by a hammer like the one found in the Bury shop.

The Assizes Court in Manchester was crowded for the trial of William Dukes

The prosecution case was a strong one and when they closed their presentation, the defence asked that the prisoner might be allowed to make a statement. Dukes then moved to the front of the dock and, in a clear firm voice, addressed the court with a statement that included the following :- "As the deceased was running at me, I put my heels behind him and threw him, and he came down on the fender with the back of his head, and in my passion and having drink in me, I really do not know what took place after. I believe I did strike him on the forehead with the hammer. It might equally have been my life that might have been taken, if I had not defended myself".

Generally, though, the evidence presented did not in any way confirm the assertion of Dukes that the act was committed in self defence. On the contrary it showed that the victim had been subjected to brutish violence.

In fact, the jury took less than fifteen minutes to return a 'Guilty' verdict after the two day trial. His Lordship then passed sentence of death, urging the prisoner to prepare for the ordeal ahead.

The execution of William Dukes took place three weeks later on Christmas Eve, 1889, at Strangeways Gaol. During his last night he slept little, being very restless and he woke early in the morning. He ate a fairly good breakfast and as the hour fixed for execution approached, he did not flinch.

He looked pale when he appeared on the scaffold shortly after eight o'clock that morning. He asked James Berry, the executioner, if he could speak and, addressing the reporters gathered below in the prison yard, he said, "Tell my wife that I die happy". It was raining heavily at the time, and when the bolt was drawn water splashed from the platform into the well beneath. He died without a tremor, and there was a marked absence of muscular twitching after death.

It was revealed later that Dukes had left no statement beyond that which he made at the trial, when he claimed that Gordon first attacked him.

Chapter 31

A Deadly Poison Administered

On Tuesday, March 24th 1835, John Orrell aged 40, of Bolton-le-Moors appeared at the Lancaster Spring Assizes charged with the wilful murder of Elizabeth Orrell, a child of tender age. He was accused of causing her death by making her drink or swallow a certain deadly poison called white arsenic.

The case excited more interest than any at that Assizes and the court was crowded throughout the day. When the proceedings began the prosecution outlined briefly the circumstances leading up to the alleged crime.

The mother had died on the 4th of February and had been buried a week later. The accused at the time had been living at Barrow Bridge, about two miles from Bolton, but following the death of his wife he collected his two youngest children from their grandparents and set up home for them in a rented cellar at Bolton, close to the home of his uncle. Within days of John Orrell's arrival he was knocking on his uncle's door informing him that six-year-old William had died, and that eight-year-old Elizabeth was poorly.

The boy was buried on the following Tuesday and the young girl was still poorly. The next day she was no better being very ill and vomiting, then during the night she passed away. The uncle of the accused was present at that time and said it would be best to get a doctor, but Orrell declined saying he had no money.

The death of two apparently previously healthy children aroused natural suspicion and following the daughter's death a search was made of the cellar.

During that search a local constable discovered a parcel resting on a ceiling beam between two joists. The parcel was about eight feet from the floor and could be reached without standing on a chair.

The court heard how the contents of the parcel were examined and it was found to contain arsenic. A subsequent post-mortem examination of the girl's body revealed a large amount of the same substance and all the evidence pointed to her having been killed through administration of the deadly poison.

At this stage of the trial several witnesses were called who were fellow prisoners with the accused in 1831 and 1832 when he spent a number of months in Lancaster Castle in connection with debts. They recalled how he had frequently spoke of his wife and the two youngest children stating that he would destroy them. He had spoken of his wife's infidelity and claimed that she was the mother of bastard children.

Hanging Corner at Lancaster Castle - scene of John Orrell's execution

During his months in prison the surgeon of the Castle had frequently examined him and on a number of occasions it had been recorded that he behaved in an insane manner. However, it had been concluded that when released in June 1832, he was behaving in a rational manner.

At the outset of the proceedings Orrell had been undefended but midway through the trial Dr Brown, who was one of those called to give medical opinion, agreed to undertake the accused man's defence.

When all the evidence had been presented the learned Judge then charged the jury, summing up the whole proceedings in a most lucid and forcible manner, omitting no point that could possibly be construed in favour of the prisoner.

The jury then retired for a few minutes and when they returned they delivered a verdict of Guilty against John Orrell.

His Lordship then pronounced sentence upon the prisoner in a most impressive and feeling address. There could exist, he said, no doubt in reasonable minds of his guilt of the awful crime of which he was convicted. He had alleged that those children were not his own; but whether or not, they were of tender years; they had never offended him and he ought under the circumstances to have sheltered and protected them.

There were, the Judge continued, other suspicions against him. Whether or not he had also destroyed his wife and other child, his own conscience would tell him.

He then went on to sentence Orrell to death, and remarked that such a sentence was fitting for such an aggressive crime.

John Orrell's remaining time was short and on the following Thursday morning, shortly after eight o'clock he was executed. He was said to have evinced no want of firmness on the awful occasion, but he did not address the people assembled to witness his death.

It is recorded that up to the moment of his conviction he had entertained a confident expectation of an acquittal, and that up to the last moment he persisted in asserting his innocence of the crime for which he died.

Chapter 32

Gaol Breaker's Short-lived Freedom

Towards the end of March 1888, a stranger appeared amongst the inhabitants of Eccles, near Manchester and within a few days was making enquiries respecting Alfred Poynter, a captain in the Salvation Army. Suspicions were aroused and in consequence a local police constable, by the name of Crowther, concealed himself in the Poynter's house on the night of the 29th of March.

Some hours later, when the family had retired to rest, the man made his appearance as his informer had predicted. He had scaled the back yard wall, effected an entry through the kitchen window, and begun work to rifle the house when the constable pounced on him. A short struggle ensued and the burglar was finally captured and found to be in possession of some formidable house-breaking implements.

When the man appeared at the Salford Sessions on the 9th of April, he pleaded guilty and under the name of John Jackson, aged 33, a plumber by trade he was given a six month prison sentence with hard labour. The Eccles burglary was deemed to be his first offence and the sentence passed reflected that presumption.

After sentencing, the man became an inmate of Strangeways Gaol and in accordance with the custom of the establishment, was kept for a month in close confinement and employed in cotton or oakum picking. Being exceedingly well behaved during that time he was, a month later by the Governor's direction, transferred to the blacksmith's shop.

Some little time afterwards Mr Preston, the Governor, received a complaint respecting a smell of gas in the house of Miss Little, the matron, and he accordingly gave instructions that the place should be examined by a plumber to ascertain where the leakage occurred. Accordingly, Jackson was sent there, under the charge of a warder. His first visit took place on the afternoon of Saturday, May 19th and he was sent there again on the Monday and on the Tuesday morning.

The task required a further visit on the Tuesday afternoon and on that occasion Jackson was entrusted to the charge of assistant warder Ralph Dyer Webb. The officer, who was in his mid forties and a steady, quiet, kindly disposed man, seemed to be on exceptionally good terms with the prisoner. Shortly before four o'clock that afternoon the two men went into the matron's bedroom to examine and repair the piping. By this time Miss Little was home and relaxing in her sitting room below.

After a minute or two, the matron heard what she later described as a rumbling noise, like the moving of furniture. She went at once to the bedroom and to her surprise found the door locked. Twice she shook the door and demanded admittance. Receiving a negative response to her request she at once hurried from the house to raise the alarm.

Within minutes several warders had responded and the door of the bedroom was burst open, a terrible spectacle being presented to the men as they entered the room. Webb was discovered lying on the floor in a pool of blood, divested of his boots and with a terrible wound on the left side of his head, just above the ear. His coat was unbuttoned and his trouser pockets were turned inside out. Jackson was nowhere to be seen, but his disappearance was easily explained, for in the ceiling at the right corner of the room, just over the wardrobe, was a large hole which had not been there before.

It was manifest that the prisoner had escaped by that means, and on the discovery being made the alarm bell was rung, men being sent out in all directions to search for the fugitive. Despite the prompt attention of the warders', Jackson, dressed in prison garb, managed to get clean away.

Meanwhile, every possible assistance was given to the unfortunate Webb, who was shortly afterwards roused to semi-consciousness. He was unable to say what had happened to him and only made a few incoherent remarks, before lapsing into unconsciousness from which state he died a couple of hours later.

The escape of Jackson appeared to have been carefully planned and boldly executed. For the purpose of his work in the matron's house he had obtained a heavy hammer from the blacksmith's shop. This he had taken with him to the bedroom and it was apparent that the awful implement had been used to deliver the death blow. Once he had deprived the warder of consciousness he had possessed himself of his victim's pocket-knife and boots. Then using the hammer and a chisel he had broken through the ceiling, making a hole large enough to enable him to scramble on to the house roof. From there it was an easy matter for him to reach the outer wall of the prison and make the drop into Southall Street. How he then managed to pass through the heart of a crowded city in broad daylight, attired in a suit of prison clothing, without attracting attention was amazing to both the prison authorities and the police alike.

After his astonishing escapade, Jackson did not appear very careful to conceal his whereabouts. That same night he turned up in Oldham, where he committed a burglary at the home of a Salvation Army captain and stole a number of articles of clothing. This exploit he followed by breaking into another house in the neighbourhood and throughout the night the parks and outlying fields in the vicinity of Oldham, where it was thought the fugitive might sleep, were carefully searched.

Public uneasiness was intensifying and it was feared that with his bravado for burglary and his desperate situation, he may have purchased some deadly weapon. By morning the police had issued over a thousand posters which contained a description of the escaped convict, and photographs of Jackson were broadcast throughout the country.

When the hue and cry had been fully raised the authorities ascertained for the first time who and what manner of man Jackson really was. Various police records came to light and showed that instead of being a first offender, he was in fact a most inveterate, determined and dangerous criminal.

His real name was discovered to be Charles Wood Firth and he was a native of Birstall, in the West Riding of Yorkshire. Despite being educated beyond the ordinary level he had often abandoned his trade as a plumber and become a drifter.

At times he had obtained employment in Chorley, Blackburn Burnley and other east Lancashire towns, but once he had money in his pocket he was bound to spend it. From a loose, aimless kind of life he descended into the criminal courses. Eventually burglary had become the ruling passion of his life and at times he had varied the pursuit with a little horse stealing and forgery.

His criminal activities did not go un-detected and prison sentences of a short duration followed. While serving one sentence at Wakefield Gaol, in the summer of 1883, he had successfully escaped, scaling the prison wall and fleeing through the town un-detected. On that occasion he left the country and travelled to Africa, returning to familiar haunts around Bradford a year later, ending up once more in police hands and being given a prison term for his earlier gaol break. That spell in Armley Gaol, Leeds was followed by a period of wandering from town to town.

For a short period in his formative years, Jackson had been a prominent member of the Salvation Army in his native town, his talent as a vocalist being much admired. It appeared that he had developed a grievance against the organisation and taken a delight in victimising members. One such exploit leading to his earlier incarceration inside the walls of Strangeways Gaol.

Despite strenuous police activity Jackson continued to evade recapture. Reports flooded in from every quarter claiming sightings in one locality or another, but all turned out to be false. In all, the fugitive that everybody was on the look-out for, succeeded in eluding the police for three weeks.

His final capture was simply an accidental sequel to his predisposition for burglary. It happened on Monday, June 11th when he was apprehended attempting to break into a house in Bradford. After giving a false name, he was conveyed to the police station for questioning. Later that day two detectives realised who the man was and when he was confronted by their conclusion, he responded by saying, "Yes, I am Jackson, or Firth. I am the man that has done it. I wish I was dead. I am miserable. I should have given myself up".

The public announcement of Jackson's capture created a sense of relief and his trial in the middle of July 1888, was greeted with abnormal interest. It was held at Manchester Assizes and took place before Mr Justice Grantham. So great was the demand for admission that it was found necessary to place a cordon of police around the building. The trial lasted from ten o'clock in the morning until seven o'clock in the evening, and all the proceedings were followed with interest by a crowded court. Amongst the exhibits were the hammer used to kill the assistant warder, and a pair of prison boots bespattered with blood, which Jackson had left behind on his flight to freedom.

The only defence offered was that the unfortunate Webb had stumbled and caught the blow of the hammer accidentally as Jackson was attempting to strike the chisel.

Mr Justice Grantham gave a forceful and clear summing up and the jury took little time in bringing in a verdict of Guilty. The prisoner then being informed that he must suffer the penalty of death for the wilful murder of Ralph Dyer Webb.

As Jackson left the dock he staggered to the steps and was assisted by the warders. Once in the corridor below he appeared completely dazed and on retiring to his cell he broke down in grief. On being transferred to the condemned cell the prisoner found himself watched by two warders day and night. It was feared that although he appeared docile and repentant he may attempt self-destruction. For the first few nights after the trial he did not sleep too well, but as the day of reckoning grew nearer he appeared calmer and slept better.

An attempt was made to obtain a reprieve by those who laboured under the impression that he did not intend to kill Webb. To this end over 20,000 signatures were obtained, but the petition gained a negative response from the Home Secretary.

During his confinement the prisoner wrote letters to his parents, brothers and sisters, all were couched in the most affectionate terms and containing the assurance that he was resigned to his fate.

On the day before the execution his father travelled from Birstall to see his unfortunate son, and the scene was a most distressing one. Mr Firth was saddened to see the young man who had been a promising youth, with cultivated tastes, set to end his life on the gallows.

That night James Berry, the executioner, arrived at Strangeways Gaol and in accordance with prison regulations had to remain in the precincts of the gaol until his work was complete. The condemned cell in which Jackson resides was Cell B. No. 19 and was on the second tier of the extreme end of the wing, being close to where the scaffold was fixed. Viewed from the prison yard the scaffold was on the second floor of the gable, being fixed on slides. When properly adjusted it stood out several feet from the wall, and according to Berry it was one of the most perfect scaffolds in the Kingdom. Access was gained through doors at the end of the wing, so that the distance from the condemned cell to the scaffold was but a few yards.

When the fateful morning of Tuesday, August 7th arrived, the prisoner ate a breakfast of tea, bread and butter, but was only able to take a small portion of it. He had been exceedingly restless and never at any time during the night had been in a sound sleep, appearing to be much agitated during his slumbers. After breakfast he was visited by the Rev Dreaper the prison chaplain and the pair of them spent some considerable time in prayer.

At about fifteen minutes before eight o'clock the whole of the prison staff of warders was drawn up near to the entrance of the wing which contained the condemned cell. Then three minutes before the appointed hour, Berry entered the condemned cell with his pinioning apparatus. Jackson, who appeared very pale, was dressed in a woollen shirt, dark grey coat and vest and wore light-coloured trousers. He was resigned to his fate and quietly submitted himself to the pinioning process.

The execution party was preceded by four warders, colleagues of the victim Webb, and as they walked the sixteen paces to the scaffold, the chaplain read the solemn burial service. Below, in the prison yard were assembled prison staff and warders and, as Jackson appeared, he took a hasty glance round and then shut his eyes. Berry then shook hands with him, placed the white cap over his head, stepped back, pulled the lever and the prisoner, who weighed 10st 1lb, fell a depth of 5ft 6in. The rope appeared to twitch a couple of times and then all was quiet. For executioner Berry, the culprit was the 126th he had launched into eternity.

Chapter 33

Little Thought for Dangers of the Sea

In the middle of the nineteenth century the boat-makers of England were invited to submit entries for the construction of a lifeboat. A prize of £100 was offered by the Duke of Northumberland for the most successful competitor. It was won by the establishment of Messrs. Beechin and Son, who carried out their business in Great Yarmouth.

The craft which was adapted to either rowing or sailing was in most nautical circles highly spoken of, and pronounced capable of withstanding the most severe seas. Her superiority over other vessels was felt to be her ability to instantly self-right in the event of her being capsized.

Around this time their had been many casualties in the area around Lytham in Lancashire, with a number of vessels being wrecked. Conscious of the need for increased vigilance, a subscription was set up to purchase a lifeboat for the Lytham seafarers. Impressed by the prize winning lifeboat an order was placed with the Great Yarmouth yard.

Not everyone in the North West felt that the purchase was a good one. Indeed the lifeboat men of Liverpool were happier using a patent tubular life-boat called 'The Challenger' which was built in a Manchester shipyard. Their boat had been tested in every kind of gale and so confident were her crew that they issued a challenge to every other lifeboat in Great Britain. Initially, the designers of the prize lifeboat accepted the challenge, but after 'The Challenger' sailed down to Ramsgate they were informed that the contest was cancelled as the prize lifeboat had been sold.

Eventually in September 1852, the men from the Merseyside lifeboat had a first hand look at the new Lytham lifeboat, while on manoeuvres at Southport. The Lytham men laying great stress on the boat's righting herself quickly if she capsized. Their reaction riled one of the old-timers from Liverpool, who had seen the boat capsize in Prince's Basin at an earlier trial, before the Dock Committee. In no uncertain terms he remarked to those present, in good broad old

Lancashire, "Capsizing as won't capsize. I tells you that there boat will drown you all the first time you go out with any sea on, she will for sure".

The Lytham men, though, were happy with their vessel and on the first Friday of October in 1852 they gathered at midday before high water, and with only a 'fresh breeze' to contend with they set out for practice, leaving behind the life belts.

They set out with oars, and had no sail up, but in about a quarter of an hour under the direction of William Swann, the Captain of the lifeboat, the sail was hoisted. The wind started to freshen up and while they were beating down the channel the wind increased into almost a hurricane. The lower reef of the lug sail was taken in but before further action could be taken, a sudden gust of wind caught the sail, which filled with water and the boat capsized; the Captain and the other nine ill-fated occupants being hurled into the deep. A number of the men managed to cling on to the grating and seats of the vessel or the man-rope which circumscribed the boat.

The place where the occurrence took place was about two and a half miles from the lighthouse, off the Horse Bank, where the depth of water when the tide was out, was four yards.

After the accident the wind moderated very considerably and the boat was spotted from the hills, and she was then keel uppermost. An alarm was instantly given, and from end to end the village was filled with excitement, which increased as the time wore on. Two boats were got ready as speedily as possible and taken to the scene of the disaster. The smaller craft was moored at the edge of the Horse Bank, and the crew hastened across the bank, plunged into the channel, and swam to the life-boat.

The catastrophe had occurred at a half past one, and by this time it was nearing six o'clock. For those long hours members of the crew had fought to keep themselves above the water. One by one they had fallen to tired nature and, thoroughly exhausted, been washed away by the waves.

The captain, William Swann, had been ascending the outside of the boat when a surging breaker had washed him into the sea. For John Davis, George Cookson, John Gillett, John Whiteside, Thomas Hardman and James Winder, the hours of excruciating trial had ended in a watery grave in the company of their captain.

Only two men were still holding on to the gratings of the vessel

Life-Belt.—During the storm of the 9th of February, the Whitby life-boat capsized, when twelve out of thirteen of her crew perished. The man saved was the only one who had on an efficient life-belt, of which the accompanying drawing is a representation:—

This belt is on the plan of Capt. Ward, R.N., Inspector of Life-boats to the National Life-boat Institution, and is always worn on every occasion of service or exercise of its life-boats, by each man forming the crew. The Whitby life-boat establishment is now in connection with the Institution.—*The Life-boat Journal.*

Furious Driving in the Streets.—Between the month of January, 1858, and March, 1860, no less than 1457 persons had been run over in the metropolitan district and seriously injured, 170 of whom had been killed. In the City of London, during the same period, 370 persons had been driven over and injured, 30 of whom had died from their injuries.

The importance of the new life-belts was known to all – yet the crew of 1852 left theirs behind

when the rescuers arrived. They were Richard Gillett and James Parkinson. Richard Gillett informed the men that his brother Thomas had slipped into the sea only fifteen minutes before their arrival.

The survivors were at once taken back to Lytham and, as they arrived, the agony of those whose relatives did not return was beyond description, all eight of the Lytham seafarers leaving behind a widow and children. In all, twenty six children were bereaved and six of those were the youngsters of Thomas Hardman.

The following morning the bodies of George Cookson and Thomas Gillett were washed up on the Middle Bank, a short distance from where the occurrence took place and twenty-four hours later, the corpse of John Davis was discovered some three miles distant in Croston Pool. Within days five more bodies of the unfortunate sailors were washed up at Southport.

An inquest was held at the Ship Inn, Lytham at which the accident was mainly ascribed to the super-abundant quantity of sail carried, to which a charge of carelessness was established against the captain. He had been anxious to see what the boat could do and he disregarded the other crew members who urged him to take in some sail.

It was also pointed out that the seamen had not acted according to rule, having left behind their life-belts. An act of negligence, which they undertook despite being cautioned by a local clergyman to not go without them.

The captain had been attempting to right the vessel when he was washed away and the surviving sailors spoke of their skipper as a good seaman. After consultation with the coroner the Jury brought forward a verdict of "Accidentally drowned", so ending a grievous and heartrending calamity which, once again, highlighted the dangers of the sea. By a cruel twist of fate the words of the old-timer from Liverpool had become only too true.

The monument at Lytham St Anne's recalls a gallant rescue attempt by the life-belt clad crew in 1886

Postscript: The ill-fated lifeboat was named 'ELEANOR CECILY' after the young wife of John Talbot Clifton, the Squire of Lytham. Within three months another gallant crew had been assembled to man the lifeboat and they were soon called to action to effect a rescue on the Salthouse Bank.

In 1854 the Royal National Lifeboat Institution took over the station and they refitted the 'Eleanor Cecily' and named her 'The Wakefield'.

Chapter 34

Farewell to Beauty and Innocence

In 1838 in a small hamlet called Fairhurst, in the township of Goosnargh; between 8 and 9 miles from Preston and about 6 miles from Garstang, lived the Sanderson family. The family consisted of Ann Sanderson, her husband Edward and their five children Eleanor aged 12, James aged 9, Margaret aged 6, Robert aged 4 and William just 2 years old. They resided in an old white cottage, which they had occupied for some years.

Edward Sanderson was respected for his sobriety, industry and general good conduct; while his wife was remarkable for her pre-possessing appearance, her inordinate pride, her love of dress, her ambition to outstrip her neighbours in appearance and her invariable discontent and repining at the narrowness of her means. The five children had nothing to distinguish them, save their personal beauty which many described as extraordinary.

The Sanderson's had been married for about thirteen years and had started their wedded life in a dwelling at Skerton, with the husband being employed as a day labourer at Quernmore. Ann Sanderson looked well after their home and took in knitting and sewing to supplement their income. Eventually she became discontented with the humility of her station, and desirous of improving her prospects, and bettering her circumstances, she prevailed upon her mother who lived in Ambleside to lend her ten pounds with which she set her husband up in the business of a butcher.

In the business they were unfortunate and lost money, forcing them to move into Goosnargh, and at Fairhurst they commenced shop-keeping. Fortune once again frowned upon them and they became involved in debt. The conduct of the wife become marked by a degree of strangeness and eccentricity. Such being her behaviour that on the 18th of May 1838, she left her husband and family and, taking with her the youngest child, went off to Manchester where her brother resided.

Within a couple of months she had returned to Fairhurst announcing that her brother, who was a soldier, had died of cholera and his wife had hastily married another man. Sanderson, who had never rebuked nor chided her for her long absence, merely told her, "stop your wanderings, become settled and I shall forgive you".

To Sanderson it appeared as though his wife was resigned to caring for their family and to pay for the upkeep of the house he got a job locally as a day labourer. In fact to his employment he went quite cheerfully on the first Thursday of September 1838, unaware of the tragedy that lay in store in the home he left behind.

At about half past twelve on that day John Brewer, who resided at Little Inglewhite, was passing Sanderson's house when he was called in by Mrs Sanderson, the woman telling him that she and the children had eaten some pudding for dinner and that she was afraid there was something in it which had poisoned them.

When he went into the house he noticed all the children looking very ill. There was flour pudding upon the table and also melted butter, knifes, forks and plates. The pudding had been cut into with some parts of it upon the plates. Following a request from the woman, John Brewer then went to get medical assistance.

Within a short time two surgeons from Garstang were at the house and by half past two o'clock the husband had returned to the cottage having been informed of the tragedy. When he entered his home he found his wife and offspring surrounded by the surgeons and a number of neighbours. His wife addressed him in the most affecting manner, and in terms of nervous feeling and earnestness with regard to the awful situation of herself and her dying children.

Soon after the arrival of the surgeons a slice of the pudding was given to a duck, which died almost immediately. The medical men worked throughout the afternoon to mitigate the sufferings and to preserve the lives of the ill-fated family. Sadly, at five o'clock, four-year-old Robert died and within minutes the youngest son, William expired. Before another hour had elapsed two more children James and Margaret slipped away, after enduring a great deal of suffering. Not long after they had breathed their last the eldest child, Eleanor, also passed away. As the lifeless children lay in peace the hand of death was fast closing upon the mother. She had a ghastly, terrified and death stricken appearance as those who witnessed the horrible scene stood by in heavy emotion.

With death about to enshroud her she sent for the Rev Gradwell, the Catholic priest of Claughton Hall chapel and she told him that in consequence of her being in debt, her neighbours had turned their backs on her and that she had therefore put some arsenic into the pudding to poison herself and the children. Her release from torment and excruciating pain arrived at nine o'clock that night, to end a life of thirty two years duration.

The inquest into the tragedy took place at Inglewhite, in the Green Man Inn public house on the following Saturday. The jury consisted of some of the most respected and intelligent individuals in the township. Prior to the inquest they had to visit the cottage to view the bodies – a duty most harrowing and filled with intense sorrow. Two beds were placed side by side – on one lay the mother and the two youngest children and on the other were deposited the mortal remains of the other three children. The six empty coffins which awaited the lovely babes and once beloved wife were piled in the centre of the room and looking on was the broken-hearted husband. He stood pale and haggard in countenance, with his eyes swimming in tears – he spoke not, the terror held him silent.

The neighbours, the surgeons and the local clergymen were all called to address the inquest and the events of the awful September afternoon horrified all present.

The Green Man, scene of the inquest into the tragedy

One of the final witnesses called was the Rev Thomas Benn, the incumbent of Whitechapel, in Goosnargh. He stated that until recently Ann Sanderson had been one of his congregation and that in the month of March she had visited his home in an agitated state. During their conversation she had told the reverend gentleman that when she and her husband were on unhappy terms, she had thought several times of destroying herself and the younger children. That visit had ended with Ann Sanderson saying that she had repented and was glad that she had.

The Rev Benn heard of the drama at the Sanderson cottage shortly after tea on the Thursday afternoon. By then, four of the children were dead and Ann Sanderson was vomiting and on the brink of death. She told him that she had taken some arsenic the day before, and that afterwards she had made up her mind that she would not leave the children behind. In the opinion of the Rev Benn the woman had not been of sane mind, her conduct for a long time being marked with low cunning.

When the coroner, Richard Palmer, summed up the case he did so with great clearness and perspicuity. The jury immediately retired from the room and after being absent a short time they returned with their verdict. It was that Ann Sanderson had been suffering from "Temporary Insanity" and that the death of the children took place as a consequence of having had poison administered to them.

The funeral of the ill-fated woman and her unfortunate children took place on the Sunday at Goosnargh. The stillness of the Sabbeth day was interrupted and the peace and quiet of the village was disturbed by the influx of traffic, the hurry of pedestrians and the constant chatter of the crowds of spectators. Over two thousand people flocked into the village from the surrounding places and by half past two o'clock that afternoon the funeral procession had reached Goosnargh.

At length the church was neared, and the minister, arrayed in his surplice, met the procession at the portals. He preceded it and commenced the service. Then was borne the coffin of the wretched woman, covered with a black pall, and supported on a bier by her sorrow-stricken husband and her sole remaining brother. Next in order came the children according to their respective ages, upon whose coffins were thrown white sheets – emblems, as it were, of their beauty and innocence. They likewise were carried on biers, by

The churchyard in the secluded and rural village of Goosnargh was selected for the interments

the boys and girls with whom they had, in the midst of life, frequented the Sunday School of Whitechapel.

There was no hearse with its sable plumes; biers had borne both parent and children from their home to the dwelling of the tomb. The father, brother and few relatives had followed them in a cart, attended by a vast concourse of both men and women, who all seemed affected by the mournful spectacle.

The church service was conducted by the Rev Studholme and during it the grieving husband was seated at the foot of his wife's coffin. Over his eyes Edward Sanderson held a white handkerchief that was bedewed with tears, and the sorrow had reached the hearts and eyes of all in attendance.

When the coffins were carried out of the church into the 'field of graves', streams of tears watered the cold clay under which they were about to be deposited. The coffin of Ann Sanderson was lowered amid sorrow and pity, rather than the censure or denunciation of thousands. Her body, and those of her sacrificed progeny, were consigned to dust and ashes and laid side by side in a grave at the north side of Goosnargh church. Owing to the numbers who pressed to see them lying in the earth, the coffins were not covered with the mould and sods until eleven o'clock that night.

"Oh the grave! – the grave!
It buries every error.
Covers every defect.
Extinguishes every wrathful sentiment".

Chapter 35

Romance, Revenge & Regrets

On the last Saturday before Easter, in 1868 two young men, Timothy Faherty and Miles Weatherill, stood on the gallows in front of the New Bailey Prison, Salford awaiting their imminent execution at the hands of the long serving public executioner, William Calcraft. The two unhappy men were set to suffer a shocking and ignominious death after committing murder in horrible and tragic circumstances.

The crime for which Faherty had been convicted had been committed on Christmas Day, 1867 at Droylsden. The victim of his savage assault being his would be sweetheart Mary Hanmer, who was six years his senior. The path of romance had not run smoothly for either Timothy Faherty, a thirty-year-old discharged soldier, who hailed from Galway in Ireland or his companion on the scaffold, 23-year-old Miles Weatherill, a cloth weaver, who had been employed at Todmorden.

Faherty had at an early age enlisted in the 40th Regiment in which he served for a term of twelve years. When the term of his enlistment expired he claimed his discharge and, after visiting some relatives in Manchester, he went to Droylsden where he obtained work as a power loom weaver. It was there that he had made the acquaintance of Mary Hanmer who was also a weaver.

From Droylesden Faherty regularly corresponded with his widowed mother in Galway and often mentioned his intention to return home for the first time since his enlistment in the army. In fact just two days before Christmas he wrote to his mother telling her that the letter would be his last before his return to see her.

However, passion was to order his fate differently because Mary Hanmer did not reciprocate the affection he bestowed upon her. He had made many attempts to ingratiate himself in her favour but each time he had met with failure. When he spoke to her of his return to Ireland and asked if she had any commands, she treated him with indifference and told him, "Give my respects to the green fields and the shamrocks of Ireland".

The utter indifference of the woman's comments to him on Christmas Day, 1867 incited Faherty to the commission of a deed that he later claimed had never previously entered his thoughts. Following her upstairs at the house where she lodged and where he had formerly lived, he struck her repeated blows with a poker. So fierce was his attack that even after she had fallen he continued to hit her, eventually fracturing her skull and causing her immediate death.

His unhappy mother heard of his arrest on the awful charge of murder on the very day she was expecting his return to Galway. In consequence their first meeting in thirteen years was not to take place at home but in a prison cell prior to his trial.

After his condemnation his mother and several other relatives from Galway visited him. He had about him an air of resignation and he took great notice of the religious consolations of Father Gadd. In an attempt to avert his execution it was hoped to obtain the intervention of his former commanding officer, but the reply to the application was unfavourable.

The crime for which Miles Weatherill stood condemned had taken place on the 2nd of January 1868, at the Todmorden Parsonage. The victims of his atrocious actions being the Rev Mr Plow, a servant called Jane Smith and indirectly the Rev. Plow's infant daughter.

Weatherill, whose mother was also a widow, had the reputation of being a young man of good character and conduct, if a little passionate. At one time he had been a scholar at the Wesleyan Sunday School and later he became connected with the Christ Church Sunday School. It was there that he made the acquaintance of Sarah Elizabeth Bell, who was in the service of the Rev Mr Plow at Todmorden Parsonage. As romance blossomed Weatherill became a frequent visitor to the Parsonage, eager to be in the company of young Sarah.

The courtship was not approved of by Mr and Mrs Plow on account of the immaturity of the young lady, but it was carried on clandestinely, even after Sarah had promised her master and mistress that the intimacy would be given up. To that end Weatherill continued to visit the Parsonage even after being forbidden to do so.

As the weeks passed by he began to form an opinion that another servant, Jane Smith, had told tales to the Reverend and his wife in reference to his visits, and that she had also spoken disparagingly of him to Sarah.

Eventually, on the first day of November 1867, Sarah was forced to leave the Parsonage, in consequence of some unpleasantness

Todmorden Parsonage - scene of the brutal killings

arising from her persistent attachment to Weatherill. When he heard of Sarah's departure Weatherill was deeply offended at the necessity of her dismissal, and the blame he put on the shoulders of Jane Smith.

Without too much difficulty Sarah obtained a situation at the Friends' Retreat in York and on New Years Day, 1868 Weatherill went over to see her. During his visit he beseeched her to return to Todmorden, and when she refused to do so he declared that he would have his revenge. He departed, whispering the word, "revenge" in her ear and placing a locket around her neck, "to wear for his sake".

After leaving his sweetheart in York that Sunday evening, he returned to Todmorden having, in the meantime, possessed himself of no fewer than four pistols and a hatchet. With the tools of destruction on his person he went to the Parsonage at ten o'clock on the following night.

He knocked on the back door and at once caught the attention of Mr Plow who, on failing to open that door, exited from the front door to see who was round the back. When the reverend gentleman approached the back door he was attacked by Weatherill who was brandishing a hatchet. His cries at once roused the servants who, on reaching the back door, saw Mr Plow and his assailant in a deathly struggle.

Weatherill was still chopping at Mr Plow's head with the axe, but aided by the servants the reverend was able to escape from his attacker's grip and flee away from the house. As Mr Plow hurried to give the alarm, Weatherill turned his attention to Jane Smith and following her into the dining room, he coolly shot her dead. He then climbed the stairs and entered the bedroom of Mrs Plow, who had been recently confined, and had her week old infant by her beside in a cradle. Ignoring the crying baby he continued his vicious rampage by striking Mrs Plow across the face with a poker, smashing her nose.

Within an instant several people had rushed to the Parsonage and before he could inflict any more damage, Weatherill was secured. He appeared to be quite sober and displayed a callous indifference to his actions. His actions had not only resulted in the death of the woman against whom he sought revenge but would eventually lead to two further deaths. At first the Rev. Plow appeared to rally from his injuries but after his appearance at the Inquest he went into decline, dying on the 13th of March. With Mrs Plow being nursed to recovery her delicate infant daughter, Hilda Catherine, was deprived of her mother's care and also died that day.

As the wheels of justice brought him closer to his day of destiny Weatherill became aware of his awful position. Eventually, he expressed great sorrow for his crime and acknowledged the justice of his sentence. Two days before his execution he was visited by Sarah Bell, who was accompanied by his mother and sister. The young woman was in the deepest affliction and her grief was equalled by the prisoner's relatives.

The preparations for the executions were commenced on the Thursday when workmen began to erect the scaffold in front of the New Bailey Prison. The executioner Calcraft arrived that evening and he completed his preparations on the Friday night, in front of a large crowd of onlookers.

When Calcraft returned into the prison he was handed the following letter which had been posted for his attention:

Sir, I am write to tell you to take care; for as sure as I have a pen in my hand, you will be shot tomorrow morning about eight o'clock. I suppose you think you got home very well when you hung the FENIANS last November; but you won't get home alive again. This is plain English. There will be about 200 Fenians in the morning with loaded revolvers, ready to fire off at you; so give this up for a bad job for this time.

So look out – nothing can save you this time.

So my parting advice to you is to pray to God before you go on the scaffold. Good bye, from "A FENIAN".

In the graveyard of Christ Church, Todmorden lie the remains of the V. Rev. Plow, his child and his servant Jane Smith – victims of Miles Weatherhill's murderous revenge in March 1868.

By six o'clock on the Saturday morning there were two thousand people assembled outside the prison. As they waited they began to sing such popular melodies as, 'Glory Hallelujah', 'The Flying Trapeze', and 'John Brown'. The choruses were joined in lustily with evidently no feeling for the prisoners who were within earshot of their yellings.

When the early trains began to arrive, large crowds were seen hurrying down the streets and pushing their way to secure a good place. The main interest seemed to be concentrated on the convict Weatherill, and those persons who had arrived from Todmorden were eagerly questioned as to the former history of the murderer. There were many cries of "Sarah" from the crowd; and bets were freely offered and taken as to how Weatherill would conduct himself on the scaffold, the prevailing opinion being that he would die unflinching and without remorse.

The crowd at this time was of a motley description. There was a sprinkling of well dressed and evidently respectable persons, a number of flashily dressed women, but the majority were factory operatives and nondescripts. Adjacent windows began to fill and soon every spot which afforded a glimpse of the scaffold was occupied.

The information relative to the death threat against Calcraft was circulated shortly before execution time and this caused considerable excitement as well as an opportunity for further bets to be laid.

As the appointed hour approached close on twenty thousand persons had gathered and at a minute before eight o'clock the door at the back of the scaffold opened. There was cry of, "Hats off", from those assembled. Faherty stepped first on to the platform. He was deadly pale and his lips moved convulsively, as if engaged in earnest prayer. Behind him was Father Gadd who had been his comforter during his final days and dutifully he read the burial service. Calcraft then drew the cap over Faherty's face, placed the rope round his neck and adjusted it over the beam. Once in position the condemned man stood firm and unflinching.

Several minutes then elapsed before Weatherill entered onto the scaffold and he also appeared pale looking up towards the heavens. He walked with a firm step and stood calmly during the time Calcraft was making the preparations. He clasped firmly in his hand a prayer book which was produced at the trial, and which contained a photograph of Sarah Bell.

Calcraft then shook the hand of both men before supervising the drawing of the bolt and their fall into eternity. Faherty struggled for about two minutes and his companion in death for a somewhat longer period. From within the crowd there was fainting and screaming as the drop fell and many lingered for an hour until the bodies were cut down.

For Calcraft it had been another date in a busy schedule – by now he had become accustomed to death threats. His charge on this occasion to the County Sheriff was £20 – the fee being £10 per execution carried out.

Chapter 36

Slaying of the Sisters

At the Liverpool Assizes in the middle of November 1886, James Mellor aged 67, was put on trial for the wilful murder of his wife Sarah, and his sister-in-law Betty Kent at their home in Cecil Street, Lytham. Mellor, his wife and his wife's sister shared the house with a Mr and Mrs Whittaker, who had apartments there.

On the second day of November the Whittakers had left the house to go for a walk and, shortly afterwards, Miss Kent went to a neighbours to borrow a clothes prop. Mrs Mellor, as was her custom in the afternoon, lay down on the kitchen sofa and went to sleep.

What followed was to lead to James Mellor's appearance in the dock before Mr Justice Day. Taking up a large blacksmith's hammer, Mellor battered in the head of his sleeping wife. He then went into the garden and called Miss Kent from the neighbour's house. As soon as she returned he attacked her with the same weapon and she fell in the garden, battered about the head.

Leaving the house key with a neighbour he then proceeded down the street until he came upon a constable. He asked the police officer to return with him to his house as there were two women there who had hurt themselves.

On entering the premises the constable found Mrs Mellor lying on the kitchen sofa, face upwards with her arms folded. She was dead but her body was still warm. The top of her head was battered in and there was a large cut on the left cheekbone which completely penetrated it, and another on the upper lip. On the floor at the end of the sofa was a large pool of blood, and there were also blood splashes on the table cloth and on the door. There was no evidence of a struggle having taken place.

In the garden the constable discovered the body of Betty Kent. It was lying on the left side, a pool of blood surrounding the head, which was battered in on the top and right side. The right eye was also very much blackened, and the upper lip bruised. On the ground near the body there was a broken clothes line, with wet clothes upon it. In a shed close by the police officer found a large blacksmith's hammer, smeared with blood, the head of which corresponded in size with the wounds inflicted on both the women.

The constable then took Mellor into custody and the latter said, "You need not take me. I will go quietly". Afterwards, to a sergeant, Mellor remarked, "I am very sorry for what I have done. I hope you will forgive me".

Within days of Mellor's committal for the crime, a committee for his defence had been organised at Lytham. Subscriptions had been flowing in pretty freely when it was announced that relatives of the accused had already got the matter in hand. The committee, all of whom had known the prisoner for a number of years, were about to put forward as the defence, a story of a weak mind roused into insane frenzy by repeated acts of ill treatment over a number of years.

One gentleman writing from Ashton-Under-Lyne to the defence committee described the unhappy life that Mellor had endured with his wife in that town.

Prior to his trial Mellor had numerous visitors to Kirkdale Gaol, his place of confinement and he made no attempt to conceal anything. He told them that on the morning of the murder he quarrelled with his wife and again at noon, and that in the afternoon, while she lay asleep on the sofa, he was seized with an uncontrollable impulse to kill her. After the slaying of his wife he had decided to make away with her sister whom he regarded with more terror than his spouse.

The circumstances behind the terrible tragedy unfolded as the trial got underway. The accused had been married to Sarah Mellor for almost forty years and up to 1875 they had lived in the neighbourhood of Ashton-Under-Lyne, where Mellor was employed as a blacksmith. In that year he had met with an unfortunate accident when he fell through a roof. Such were his injuries that he was incapacitated from regularly following his employment.

Subsequently he and his wife removed to Lytham, where the accused was employed by the Railway Company, and occasionally he also followed his occupation at the local gas works. It was stated that from the time of the accident Mellor was not quite the man he had been before. From time to time he appeared to have suffered from some sort of mental disturbance and the jury were asked to consider whether the disturbance was of such character as to relieve the prisoner from responsibility for what he had done.

A great deal of medical evidence was produced to suggest that

Cecil Street, Lytham – residents were stunned by the events of November, 1886.

Mellor was insane, both by the medical experts who considered his reaction to the crime and by his sons, who related the change following his accident. He seemed to feel that both his wife and sister-in-law were hatching a scheme to get rid of him and he had a feeling of constant persecution regarding his household affairs. At times he had been very violent and living under the delusion that everybody was working against him.

The eldest son told the court of the unaccountable strangeness in his father's actions ever since the time of the accident and said that before that time things had been happy and comfortable at home.

The jury were told by the Defence Counsel that they would be very slow indeed to find the prisoner sane when he committed the frightful deed.

His Lordship in his summing up stated that the prisoner committed the offences, of that there was no doubt. He then defined the legal meaning of the word 'insanity' and warned the jury that they must not suppose that mere violence of temper was in the legal sense insanity.

During the Judge's address Mellor leaned forward in the dock and endeavoured to catch every word that fell from Mr Justice Day's lips. Throughout the whole proceedings the accused man had remained calm and collected despite the gaze of a crowded court.

The jury considered their verdict for only a few moments and then the foreman announced that they found the prisoner guilty of the killings, but not responsible for his actions. The clerk of the Crown then said, "Then you find him not guilty on the ground of insanity?" To which question the foreman replied, "Yes".

His Lordship then informed Mellor that he would be confined during Her Majesty's Pleasure, and he was at once removed from the dock.

Chapter 37

A Jealous Husband's Tragic Deeds

Just before midnight on the 23rd April 1896, the local police were called to a house in North Street, Nelson. When the constables arrived they saw Elizabeth Ann Hartley clinging to the sill of an upper bedroom window and crying out for help. The front door of the house was bolted, but with the assistance of a passer-by the officer's broke the downstairs window and entering the premises they dashed upstairs.

Making their way to the main bedroom they found some clothing burning on the bedroom floor and the room full of smoke. One of the constables immediately pulled up the window and rescued Mrs Hartley from her perilous position. As the other constable extinguished the fire he observed an infant child lying on the bed. The youngster was immediately removed from the room and taken to a neighbouring house.

A local doctor was soon on the scene and attempted to comfort the woman who was bleeding from four or five gunshot wounds to her head, neck and shoulder. Her injuries were dressed and she was made as comfortable as possible.

A search was started straight away to discover the whereabouts of her assailant, Hargreaves Hartley, the husband of the distraught woman. Apparently the husband had accused his wife of being too familiar with a painter who had been working in the house and had told her he would put an end to it.

The couple had been married about four years and Hargreaves Hartley was regarded by those who knew him as a man with a jealous disposition, who frequently caused unpleasant disturbances. There had been little cause, however, to suspect that he would attempt to take his wife's life.

During their search of the premises the police found a six-chambered revolver besmeared with blood behind the door of the back bedroom. Near the window of the main bedroom three discharged cartridges were discovered along with a rolling pin. Also found in the house was a letter, the contents of which pointed to jealousy as the cause of the tragedy.

A strict watch was kept throughout the night on several houses where Hartley might have been expected to call. He did not appear and the reason for his absence was explained at half past five the next morning. It was then that a local policeman spotted a dark cloth gentlemen's waistcoat lying on the side of the nearby stretch of the Leeds to Liverpool canal. In the pocket of the waistcoat were six loaded cartridges, similar to the one's found in the house.

The police at once set about dragging the canal and within half an hour they had discovered the husband's body. There were no signs of violence on the body of the 25-year-old weaver. It appeared that after the incident at home he had run straight down to the canal and thrown himself in. Evidently wishing to be rid of his short life and no doubt believing that he had ended his partner's existence.

In fact the life of 22-year-old Elizabeth Ann Hartley hung in the balance for over a fortnight. For some time after the occurrence she remained in a critical condition before taking a turn for the better. An attempt was made to locate the bullets, which remained inside her, by means of the latest photographic techniques. They were successfully located but no attempt was made to recover them due to the young woman's weak condition. Sadly, on the 8th of May 1896, her condition worsened and the following morning she departed from this life. A girl of determined spirit she had been hopeful of recovery, but fate decreed that she would join her tragic husband in eternity.

Chapter 38

Cruelly Butchered by a Monster

Towards the end of March 1849, the 'Liverpool Mercury' newspaper announced to its readers that the annals of crime in that town had been stained by one of the most foul and bloody deeds which it had recorded. At mid-day, near one of the crowded thoroughfares, surrounded by houses on every side, a lady, far advanced in pregnancy, her two children and a waiting maid, had been cruelly butchered by a monster in human shape. The two children were dead. Of the recovery of the mother no hope was entertained and it was thought barely possible that the girl would survive her injuries.

The house in which the dreadful scenes occurred was no. 20 Leveson Street, four doors from Great George Street – a highly respectable part of the town. The family consisted of Mrs Henrichson, her two sons, Henry George, aged 5 and John Alfred, a fine little fellow in his third year, and Mary Parr, the servant girl who had apparently reached her twenty-third year. Mrs Henrichson was the wife of Captain Henrichson, commander of the ship 'Duncan' belonging to a firm based at the Liverpool port. He had sailed for Calcutta in September 1848.

The relatives of Mrs Henrichson were highly respectable and of independent circumstances in Hull, from which place she had arrived some seven months previous. She was herself well educated and proficient in music, in which she gave lessons to her more immediate friends. It appeared that from the same prudential motives she was anxious to let some of her apartments.

On the Tuesday afternoon, the day before the killings, sometime between three and four o'clock, a man called at the Leveson Street house. After looking at the apartments, he agreed to take the back parlour and the top front bedroom. He said his name was Wilson and that he was a carpenter, in the employ of the Dock Estate, earning a salary of £2.10s.0d. a week.

About eight o'clock that evening Wilson returned and ordered tea. This refreshment being supplied to him, he partook of it very heartily. He spent the remainder of the evening in the house and about ten o'clock he sent for a pint of ale, and after drinking that he retired to his bedroom. Although he had said he expected his luggage to arrive at any moment, none of it appeared.

Wilson was apparently out early next morning and was busy setting up a series of extraordinary proceedings. About nine o'clock in the morning a youth, Edward McDermot, was passing along Frederick Street when he was stopped by a man who asked him to take a letter to no. 20 Leveson Street. In order that there might be no mistake, he told the youth that the house was the one which he would see him enter, and if he left the letter about five minutes later he would be given three halfpence.

The letter was directed to Mr John Wilson and the boy after waiting a few minutes rang the doorbell. The door was opened by the servant girl who took the letter and the boy informed her that it was from Mr Wilson's master. At that point Wilson appeared in the lobby, took the letter from the girl and giving the youth the money promised, shut the door.

About eleven o'clock that morning Mrs Henrichson went out to make some purchases, and amongst others, bought a quantity of potatoes. An errand boy in the employ of the shopkeeper was immediately despatched to the house in Leveson Street with the potatoes. On ringing the bell, the door was opened by a man answering the description of Wilson, who took in the basket, and closed the door, leaving the boy outside. After a short while the man opened the door again and returned the basket to the boy, who immediately went away. The man had a handkerchief tied round the lower part of his face, and the boy had noticed that his hands were covered in blood.

As he was leaving the steps he observed Mrs Henrichson coming up Leveson Street, and before he had proceeded far, he saw her enter the house, the door of which had been left open by the man.

Nothing more was seen of the inmates of the house until a neighbour saw the person known as Wilson leave in a hurried manner by the front door. He passed up towards Great George Street, wiping the perspiration from his face with a handkerchief. Two girls subsequently saw him drive off in a cab.

At about half past eleven, Mrs Henrichson had called at a shop in St. James Street and purchased a jug. It was arranged that a boy from the shop would deliver it within half an hour. On arriving at the house he rang the bell and knocked several times. Finding that no person answered either the knocking or ringing, he peeped through the keyhole and saw the legs and feet of a female, lying across the lobby.

Looking through the front parlour window, he saw the servant and a child lying on the floor, and immediately hastened for his master. A young lady, a pupil of Mrs Henrichson, came up at the same moment and looking in the window, burst into tears. Moans were heard to proceed from the parlour and these having attracted the attention of a neighbour, and some workmen, they determined to at once effect an entrance through the window. Breaking a pane of glass, and removing the catch of the window, an entry was obtained.

The appalling spectacle which presented itself to the men who entered was sufficient to overcome with horror the stoutest heart. Three human beings were lying on the floor, literally weltering in a pool of their own blood, their skulls and faces mutilated in the most frightful manner. The wife of an absent husband, who in a few days was expected to bear a child, lay with her head inside the parlour door and her feet across the lobby. Her hair was dishevelled, her features distorted, her face covered with gore and blood was still streaming from her fractured head.

In the middle of the floor lay the servant girl, and near the fireplace the eldest boy. They were all alive but dreadfully injured. No time was lost in procuring medical aid and, as the victims still breathed, they were conveyed to the Southern Hospital.

On further searching the house, blood was traced down into the kitchen, the walls and stairs being besmeared with it. Between the two kitchens, a large pool of the sanguineous fluid was also found, but this, to prevent observation, had been covered with a large mat. In a small pantry or closet, out of the back kitchen, was discovered the lifeless but still warm corpse of the three-year-old child. The head had been nearly severed from the body, and by its side, besmeared with blood, lay a large table knife with which the fatal wound had been inflicted. The boy was dressed in frock and petticoats, and even in death a smile seemed to play upon his innocent face. It was, indeed, a sad and heart-rending spectacle.

On going upstairs, some of the drawers and boxes in Mrs Henrichson's room were found disturbed, but to all appearances no robbery had been effected. On searching the room occupied by Wilson, marks of blood were found and it appeared as though someone had washed their hands. The water left in the basin was slightly stained as was the towel which had been used to dry his hands.

The supposed murderer was described as being in his mid-twenties, 5 feet 7 inches tall, stout built, light complexion, brown hair cut very close behind and hanging long at the sides. He was said to have been wearing a dark blue plaid sporting coat, light corded trousers, wide at the bottom, quarter Wellington boots and crepe on his hat. His hands were white and apparently unaccustomed to hard work. He had all the appearance of a sporting character, or a member of the prize-ring.

Every attention was given to the three victims taken to the Southern Hospital. Mrs Henrichson was perfectly insensible when she arrived at the hospital and she remained in that state until she passed away on the Thursday night.

The boy, Henry George, had been dreadfully beaten, he never rallied and in the course of the afternoon, died.

Mary Parr, the servant, had also been insensible when she arrived at the hospital, but she afterwards rallied and was able to give an account of the affair. Her statement was to the effect that on the Wednesday morning the eldest boy, during the absence of his mother, went into the back parlour, the apartment occupied by the man. She had requested the child to leave the front parlour while she cleaned it. What took place in the back parlour she did not know, but the little fellow soon after came running into the front parlour followed by Wilson, who struck him. The girl told the man he must not do that, as her mistress would not allow anyone to strike her children. Wilson immediately took up the tongs and felled her to the ground. Whether the blow was repeated she could not tell, but she remembered the man striking the eldest boy again, and afterwards hearing the youngest child scream. That was all that she was conscious of occurring.

The search for Wilson was soon underway and his description was circulated. He had been seen in the Crown Street area, around about twelve-thirty, washing his shoes and using a handkerchief to wipe his trousers. When he had gone, the man who observed him saw that he had left behind the blood-stained handkerchief and the letter which had been delivered to him that morning. When opened, the letter was found to be a sheet of paper with a number of lines of scribbled writing. He was next traced to a pawnbrokers shop in Great Homer Street, where he purchased a pair of blue cloth trousers. His light coloured trousers he afterwards presented to a pavior who was at work in the street.

The police were close to apprehending him throughout the day, with sightings made at various places. The next day they were just as diligent in their search and a little after nine o'clock he was taken into custody at the Police-Office in the High Street. The man had been several times during the day at a shop in Great Howard Street, offering a gold watch for sale. The shop owner, Mr Samuel, suspected that the watch had been obtained dishonestly and asked the man to accompany him to the Police-Office. This he consented to do, and when he reached the office his general appearance raised the suspicion that he was the man for whom such anxious search had been made. His dress was changed however. Instead of a hat he wore a cap, he had a pair of new blue trousers, new stockings and in his pocket was a new silk handkerchief.

Generally though, the description answered that of the man wanted for questioning. He had a wild and confused look, and appeared somewhat in liquor. He said his name was John Gleeson Wilson and that he was an engineer.

First thing the following morning the man was taken to the Southern Hospital, where it was hoped the servant girl would identify him. Along with some other men he was ushered into the room and when her eyes set upon him she said in a distinct voice, "That is the man".

By the time the trial of John Gleeson Wilson took place on Wednesday, August 22nd the servant girl had died from her wounds and her death was added to those of Mrs Henrichson and her two children. Places in the court-room were at a premium and persons of respectability and standing in the town were there to see the prisoner admitted to court. He looked well and stepped lightly up to the bar, apparently unconcerned at the awful position in which he stood. After the indictment had been read, he replied in a strong Irish brogue "Not Guilty".

The weight of evidence implicating the accused was considerable, both relative to the crime and his behaviour afterwards. The main hope of saving the prisoner's life seemed to lay in the Defence Counsel's claim that the murderer's actions were more like those of a madman than that of a rational being.

When his Lordship summed up he completely dismissed the possibility of insanity and advised the Jury that their main concern was to determine whether the prisoner at the bar had committed the barbarous murders.

The Jury, when desired to consider their verdict, discussed the case for five minutes and, without leaving the box, announced a 'Guilty' verdict. The prisoner was asked why sentence of death should not be passed upon him and he replied with a mostly incoherent utterance,

THE LIVERPOOL TRAGEDIES

Come all you feeling Christians and listen unto me,
The like was not recorded in British history,
It is of four dreadful murders committed, I am told,
By one John Gleeson Wilson, for the sake of cursed gold.

On Wednesday the 28th, consternation did prevail,
In Leveson Street in Liverpool, where thousands did bewail,
The fate of this poor family, who we are left to deplore,
Snatched from a father's fond embraces, who never will see them more.

This monster in human shape did go there to dwell
And that he went for plunder to all it is known full well,
And when this callous villain saw their defenceless state,
He did resolve them all to kill and rob them of the plate.

His bloody work he did commence all in the open day,
By striking at the children while their mother was away,
The servant girl did interfere, said, "should not do so."
Then with a poker in his hand he gave her a severe blow.

Numberless times he did her strike till she could no longer stand,
The blood did flow profusely from her wounds, and did him brand,
Then the eldest boy of five years old, in suplication said,
"Oh master, spare our precious lives, don't serve us like the maid."

This darling child of five years old he brutally did kill,
Regardless of its tender cries, its precious blood did spill,
The youngest child to the kitchen ran, to shun the awful knife,
This villain followed after and took its precious life.

A surgeon thus describes the scene presented to his view,
A more appalling case than this he says he never knew,
Four human beings on the floor all weltering in their gore,
The sight was sickening to behold on entering the door.

The mother's wound three inches deep upon her head and face,
And pools of blood as thick as mud, from all of them could trace,
None could identify the boy, his head was like a jelly;
This tragedy is worse by far than Greenacre or Kelly.

To the hospital in this sad state they quickly were conveyed,
The mother with her infant dear, and faithful servant maid,
Thousands did besiege the gates, their fate for to enquire,
But in three days from incise wounds, both of them did expire.

It will cause the captain many a pang to know their awful doom,
His loving wife and children sent to an untimely tomb,
It will make his hair turn grey with grief, no skill their lives could save,
And he did go, borne down with woe, in sorrow to the grave.

But now he is taken for this deed, bound down in irons strong,
In Kirkdale Jail he now does lie, till his trial it comes on,
May God above receive the souls of those whom he has slain,
And may they all in heavenly bliss for ever with him reign.

the thrust of it being that he was an innocent man and that sometime in the future the real criminal may be found.

His Lordship then passed sentence of death informing the prisoner that there was no possibility of his life being spared.

Two weeks later, the 'Duncan', the ship captained by Captain Henrichson, whose wife and children had been slain by Wilson, entered the Mersey. As soon as the ship entered the river three respectable gentlemen, all acquaintances of the Captain, boarded the vessel. The duty of conveying the sad intelligence did not need fulfilling, as he had been informed as soon as he had laid anchor at St. Helena.

The 'Duncan' occupied fifty nine days in returning from St. Helena to Liverpool and, during the voyage, the esteemed Captain was subjected to paroxysms of the deepest grief. Also on board the vessel had been the son of the servant girl, Mary Parr, and the news at St. Helena bore sadness to him also, for he had lost a mother.

In Kirkdale Gaol, Gleeson Wilson still continued to exhibit the same obduracy and sullen obstinacy which he had displayed since the moment he was arrested. There were always, day and night, two keepers with him and he displayed a great deal of cunning, often pretending to be asleep when actually awake.

After a couple of weeks he was removed to another cell with his previous cell undergoing the process of 'whitewashing'. On enquiring the cause of the removal the officers told him it was to prevent cholera. To which he replied, "I wish to God the cholera had come, I should like it to take me off".

When he was told that his execution was set for the following Saturday, he remarked, "Oh, why do they not hang me at once. I'm tired of waiting".

His waiting came to an end on Saturday, September the 15th, 1849 when his execution took place outside Kirkdale Gaol.

Postscript: In an attempt to rid the area of its horrific past, the name of Leveson Street was changed to Grenville Street.

Chapter 39

Sand Travellers' Short Cut to Death

It was common during the first half of the nineteenth century for travellers from Lancaster to Ulverston to take the quickest route across the sands of Morecambe Bay. The journey was only half the distance when compared with the route along land, which took in Kendal. The 'over sands' crossing was popular and daily, the time dependent upon the tide, a coach and horses ran between the two places and a stream of local carters traversed the sands.

Despite all the precautions taken, the crossing could be a hazardous one and down the years individuals and officially organised groups had been caught in the perilous shifting sands.

The arrival of the Lancaster to Ulverston railway in 1857 was to eventually sound the death knell for the stage coaches and the carters. Not, however, before the sands provided one more example of their perilous nature.

The melancholy tragedy took place over the Whitsuntide holiday in 1857. That particular weekend a group of young men, mainly farm servants, arranged to go over to Lancaster to spend their holiday with relatives and friends.

In order to make a quick return home they arranged to be conveyed by George Ashburner, aged 27, a carter employed by Mr Benson of Flookburgh. He was an experienced carter, well acquainted with the sands, making the crossing three or four times weekly.

The party left Flookburgh at about nine o'clock on the Friday night arriving at Kent's Bank within half an hour, having completed the first stage of their journey. The men then waited until ten o'clock before embarking on the sands, at a time reckoned to be a good one for the crossing.

During their stay at Kent's Bank the men visited Mr Wilcock's hotel and indulged themselves in the tap room ale. The beer was flowing freely and those present in the public bar observed that George Ashburner was more drunk than sober by the time he left.

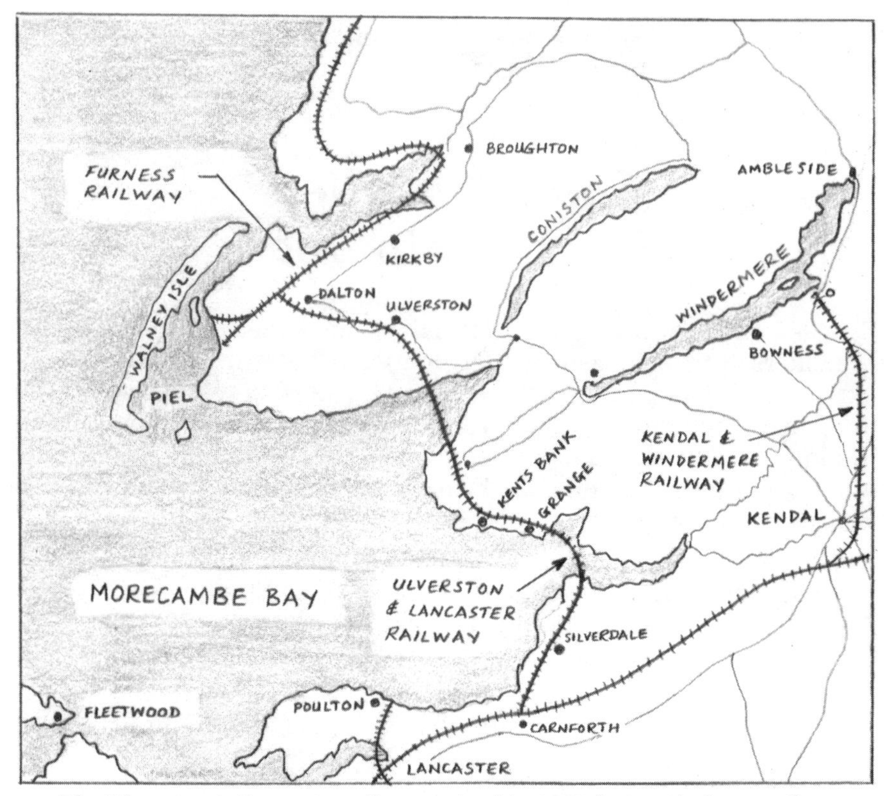

The Ulverston to Lancaster railway arrived in 1857, but not before another tragedy unfolded on the Lancaster sands

In a heavily laden cart the party was expected to make the crossing in under three hours, arriving in Lancaster in the early hours of the Saturday morning. Some of the group were anxiously awaited on the other side of the sands, but when the cart did not arrive it was assumed they had stayed the night at Kent's Bank.

In fact there was no indication of anything amiss until the Saturday afternoon when the tide moved in and some bundles and caps were washed ashore at Morecambe. A minute survey of the sands was at once made with an eye glass and attention was directed to Point Skear, where a cart was visible. As the tide moved out, a boat was despatched to the well known danger spot, some two miles from Hest Bank, which was constantly avoided by those whose occupations led them to cross the sands, as at that place there was a rock projecting out causing the eddy in the water to form a deep and dangerous hole.

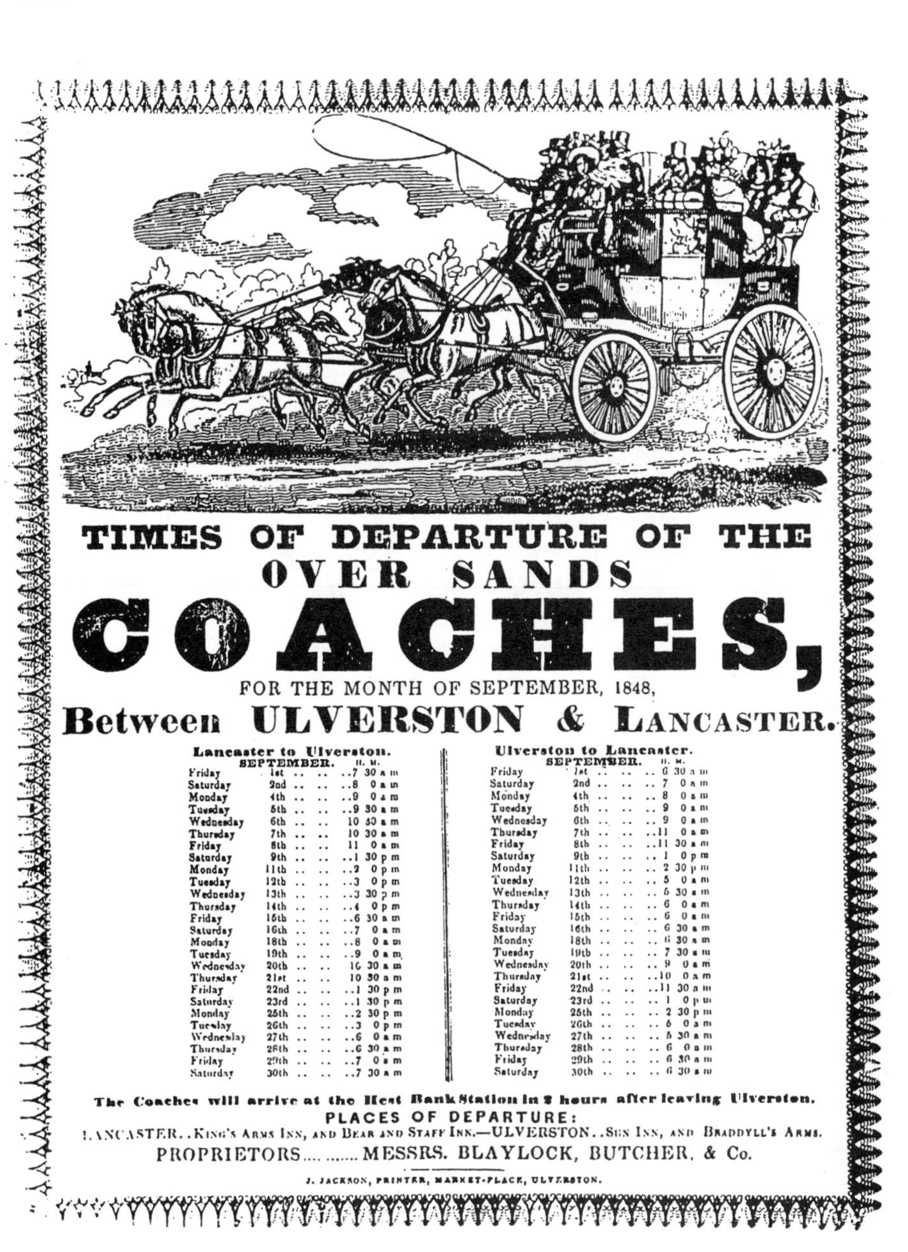

TIMES OF DEPARTURE OF THE
OVER SANDS
COACHES,
FOR THE MONTH OF SEPTEMBER, 1848,
Between ULVERSTON & LANCASTER.

Lancaster to Ulverston.

SEPTEMBER.		H. M.
Friday	1st	7 30 a m
Saturday	2nd	8 0 a m
Monday	4th	9 0 a m
Tuesday	5th	9 30 a m
Wednesday	6th	10 30 a m
Thursday	7th	10 30 a m
Friday	8th	11 0 a m
Saturday	9th	1 30 p m
Monday	11th	2 0 p m
Tuesday	12th	3 0 p m
Wednesday	13th	3 30 p m
Thursday	14th	4 0 p m
Friday	15th	6 30 a m
Saturday	16th	7 0 a m
Monday	18th	8 0 a m
Tuesday	19th	9 0 a m
Wednesday	20th	10 30 a m
Thursday	21st	10 30 a m
Friday	22nd	1 30 p m
Saturday	23rd	1 30 p m
Monday	25th	2 30 p m
Tuesday	26th	3 0 p m
Wednesday	27th	6 0 a m
Thursday	28th	6 30 a m
Friday	29th	7 0 a m
Saturday	30th	7 30 a m

Ulverston to Lancaster.

SEPTEMBER.		H. M.
Friday	1st	6 30 a m
Saturday	2nd	7 0 a m
Monday	4th	8 0 a m
Tuesday	5th	9 0 a m
Wednesday	6th	9 0 a m
Thursday	7th	11 0 a m
Friday	8th	11 30 a m
Saturday	9th	1 0 p m
Monday	11th	2 30 p m
Tuesday	12th	5 0 a m
Wednesday	13th	5 30 a m
Thursday	14th	6 0 a m
Friday	15th	6 0 a m
Saturday	16th	6 30 a m
Monday	18th	6 30 a m
Tuesday	19th	7 30 a m
Wednesday	20th	9 0 a m
Thursday	21st	10 0 a m
Friday	22nd	11 30 a m
Saturday	23rd	1 0 p m
Monday	25th	2 30 p m
Tuesday	26th	5 0 a m
Wednesday	27th	5 30 a m
Thursday	28th	6 0 a m
Friday	29th	6 30 a m
Saturday	30th	6 30 a m

The Coaches will arrive at the Hest Bank Station in 2 hours after leaving Ulverston.

PLACES OF DEPARTURE:

LANCASTER. . King's Arms Inn, and Bear and Staff Inn.—ULVERSTON. . Sun Inn, and Braddyll's Arms.

PROPRIETORS........... MESSRS. BLAYLOCK, BUTCHER, & Co.

J. JACKSON, PRINTER, MARKET-PLACE, ULVERSTON.

Copy of original poster reproduced by kind permission of Lancaster Maritime Museum and Lancashire Library, Morecambe

The inn keeper of the Morecambe Hotel, John Maudsley, was in the rowing boat that headed out to the scene and a mile and a half out they observed the body of a man in the shallow water, with his face in the sand and his plaid over his head. Next to receive their attention was the horse and cart, the animal had drowned and both horse and cart were wrong side up.

Whilst they were by the side of the cart one of the rescuers let out the cry, "Look yonder, there are the other men". Making their way along the sandy bank they came upon seven more bodies, all lying together with only twelve yards separating first to last. All were lying face down in seven or eight inches of water and some of them the sand had begun to cover.

The bodies were at once removed from the sands and taken to Morecambe to be placed in a building known as the Herring House. The place was quickly thronged by parties who had been expecting relatives and most of the bodies were soon claimed.

News of the awful occurrence soon spread and a state of gloom and consternation was apparent in the town of Lancaster and the neighbouring villages. The despair was to increase the following morning when a further search was made and two more lifeless bodies discovered.

On the Monday morning at ten o'clock an inquest was held at the North Western Hotel, Morecambe. The first duty of the jury after being sworn in, was to view the bodies of the unfortunate ten men. The fine looking young men who just a few short hours before had been in the enjoyment of robust health were laid in death. The bodies presented an appalling spectacle with their features suggesting they had been engaged in an arduous struggle to preserve life. All around the room stood relatives and friends weeping and shaking their heads in disbelief.

After the inquest had dealt with the identification issue, the story of the tragedy was pieced together. The watches of the farm hands had stopped at twenty minutes past one o'clock and taking into account the difference between real time and farm house time of one hour, it was ascertained that they had gone to their doom not long after midnight.

It appeared that George Ashburner had led the party astray by attempting to make a near cut across the sands. The jury heard how he had been drinking prior to the crossing and the feeling was that he had, in his far from sober state, made an error of judgement.

Seven of the unfortunate young men of 1857 were buried in the Poulton churchyard

The coroner stated that the tragedy was one of the most dire calamities ever to occur and he told the jury that the best verdict they could give would be an open one of "Found drowned". The jury returned a verdict accordingly.

That same afternoon, the bodies of George Ashburner, Richard Houghton and Jonathan Bell were removed home by their friends. The remaining seven, Thomas Hardman, Henry Parkinson, William Bond, William Rose, Thomas Robinson, John Williamson and John Sawyer were interred in Poulton churchyard. An immense concourse of spectators gathered to see the burial service and much sadness filled the graveyard. Thomas Hardman had been a member of the Independent Order of Oddfellows and he was followed to his grave by several members of the Order, with one of the brethren delivering the funeral oration of the Order by the side of the grave.

It was revealed later that the property on the unfortunate men, whose ages ranged from 18 years to 31, which was given up to their friends at the inquest, amounted to £48.8s.8d, three silver watches and two foreign coins.

Chapter 40

The Suffocation of Little Alice

On Monday the 12th of December 1892, a 32-year-old man named Cross Duckworth, a dressers labourer of Primrose Terrace, Bower House Fold, Witton, Blackburn appeared at the Liverpool Assizes accused of murdering nine-year-old Alice Barnes at Witton on the 8th day of November in the same year.

The court was filled and included in the crowd were a fair sprinkling of people from Blackburn. In reply to the charge Duckworth, who was an army pensioner and married with two children, said in a firm voice, "Not Guilty".

The young victim had gone to Witton Park with the cows on the fateful day and shortly afterwards she had been found in the lane close to Witton Park gates. Her death had been caused by suffocation due to a handkerchief being violently forced into her mouth as she was assaulted.

The killing had occurred about one o'clock in the afternoon and numerous witnesses were called who claimed they had seen Duckworth in the vicinity of the park gates and in the roads leading to and from the park around the time mentioned.

The landlord of the nearby Unicorn Inn gave evidence that Cross Duckworth had been in his public house from eleven o'clock and that he had left those premises at around twenty minutes to one. Whilst the landlady of another local hostelry the Turners Arms, related how Duckworth had been on their premises from the time he left the Unicorn Inn until a few minutes before one, drinking a small soda water.

A couple of other witnesses told how they had seen a man with a child in his arms. The man had let the child fall as he went through the park gates and had run off from the scene. The man had his back to these witnesses so it was not possible for them to give evidence of definite identity.

There were no shortage of other witnesses including youngsters willing to say they had seen Duckworth leaving the park area and appearing to be in a rather harassed state. The man's trousers were said to be dirty, according to those who saw him, although later superficial examination of the accused's clothing did not reveal any traces of such.

Duckworth received sentence of death

It was then recalled by the prosecution how the prisoner had been arrested on the 13th of November. The police had knocked the prisoner up and a search of the house had led to the finding of two handkerchiefs and a pair of boots.

The handkerchiefs were claimed to have been similar to the one used to suffocate the girl, while an imprint made at the scene of the crime was said to match the boot of the accused man.

The opinion was that the handkerchief was part of the same order manufactured at one place. Although not exactly alike, it was stated that a large number of these handkerchiefs had been sold.

Concerning the boots, it was said that there was a peculiarity in the boot in the way in which the nails were driven in, and that peculiarity was said to be visible in the cast.

Acquaintances of the accused revealed how he had, like most people in the neighbourhood, been interested in the developments following the crime and they claimed he had read avidly the local newspaper reports.

As the case for the defence got underway they attempted to devalue the implications suggested by the boot cast and the handkerchief, and attempted to provide an alibi for the prisoner.

The alibi was based on the accused man indulging in a full day's drinking with a couple of long standing associates, who suggested he was in conversation with them at the time of the killing. It was a tale of Duckworth being extremely drunk and his having consumed three or four special scotch whiskies before nine o'clock in the morning.

To one of these witnesses his Lordship, Mr Justice Grantham, spoke out saying, "You were drinking, drinking, drinking like a beast, drinking until you got drunk. You ought to be ashamed of yourself".

The Defence Counsel carried out a long address on the prisoner's behalf and when he concluded it he asked the jury to free their minds from prejudice and to deliberate long and hard, for it was better that this crime, despicable and cruel as it was, should go unpunished rather than the sword of justice be wrongfully used.

In his final address to the jury his Lordship went over the various crucial points; the claim that the prisoner was drinking elsewhere at the time of the crime, the fact that some of the witnesses had testified to seeing Duckworth in the vicinity of the park gates, the lack of definite proof regarding the handkerchief and the fact that 50 other boots could have made a similar imprint to the one found at the scene.

When his Lordship had finished his summing up the jury retired to consider their verdict. After an absence of an hour and in answer to the usual challenge by the Clerk, the Foreman said they found a verdict of 'Guilty', with a recommendation to mercy. In answer to the Clerk, the prisoner said "I have nothing much to say except what I have said before : I am not guilty of the crime sir".

His Lordship, in passing sentence of death, stated that the prisoner had been found guilty after a most careful inquiry by the jury, and a most able defence by the learned counsel who appeared for him and consequently he could find no fault with that verdict. Drink, he said,

EXECUTION OF THE BLACKBURN MURDERER

Cross Duckworth, who was found guilty of the murder of the little girl, Alice Barnes, at Wilton in November last, was executed on Tuesday morning in Wheaton Gaol, near Liverpool. The crime for which he suffered was a particularly brutal one, and its discovery caused a wave of horror to pass over the whole of Lancashire. More than ordinary interest, too, was excited by reason of the fact that no one actually saw the deed committed, that nearly a week elapsed before Duckworth was arrested, and that he was convicted entirely on circumstantial evidence. The story of the murder and the circumstances which led up to the arrest and conviction of Duckworth, is briefly as follows:- Alike Barnes, a fine intelligent girl, aged nine, the daughter of Edward Barnes, Redly Farm, Blackburn, left school at ten minutes past twelve, and after helping her mother a few minutes, was sent by her father to collect the cows and take them to pasture in Wilton Park. She drove the cows into the park and closed the big gates, leaving open only the wicket gate. Duckworth appears to have been watching her from a footbridge immediately in front of the gates. As the girl was returning he met her, and offered violence. To prevent the poor child from screaming the wretch thrust a handkerchief into her mouth with such force that the soft palate was torn and the root of the tongue seriously injured. The girl must have struggled desperately with her assailant. The palms of her hands were lacerated by clutching at the barbed wire fence at the side of the road. Before the man could carry out his evil designs, he was disturbed by a boy named Riding, aged ten, who saw him pick up the now apparently unconscious girl up with the object of carrying her into the lane. He fell in getting through the wicket gate, and then made off. A few minutes afterwards the girl was found dead - from suffocation - by a widow named Mart Hindi. It was not until nearly a week afterwards that Duckworth was arrested. A pair of boots was found at his house, one of which corresponded with the imprint of a heavily-nailed boot neat the scene of the struggle, and two handkerchiefs were found which it was believed at the time were of the same kind as that which had been thrust in the mouth of the victim. Duckworth could give no satisfactory account of his whereabouts on the day of the murder, but his movements were traced step by step to within three or four minutes' walk of the scene of the murder a little before the crime was committed. He was recognised by two girls as the man seen on the bridge, and the boy Riding identified him as the man he saw carrying the girl in hes arms. At the Assize trial the evidence of the boot was thrown out as unreliable, and the similarity of the handkerchiefs was doubted, leading to the abandonment of this link in the chain of evidence. The defence was an alibi, but it was not a strong one, and the Judge summed up against it. Prisoner's counsel weakened the strength of the evidence of the girls Riding and Duxbury, but that of the boy Riding remained unshaken. The jury found Duckworth guilty, but recommended him to mercy on the ground that they did mot believe he intended to commit murder. All efforts to obtain a commutation of his sentence failed. The ultimatum from the Home Secretary that the law must take its course was read to him on Saturday by Mr. Haverford, the Governor of Wheaton Gaol. Duckworth, who had all along denied knowledge of the crime and had been borne up with the hope that after the recommendation of the jury his sentence would be commuted, became terribly depressed. He slept fairly well, however, and ate his meals with something like relish. He attended assiduously to the ministrations of the chaplain, who on Monday administered the Communion to him. On the Monday afternoon, his wife, children, and other relatives visited him, and the farewell was an affecting scene. This was Duckworth's last glimpse of the outside world. A few minutes before eight o'clock on Tuesday morning, the Governor of the gaol, the chaplain, the doctor of the gaol and his assistant, the chief warder (Mr. Cunninger), and one or two gaol officials, formed in the brief and mournful death procession to the scaffold. Duckworth, who had been pinioned by Billionth, the execution, submitted to his fare like one in a dream. Punctually at eight o'clock the bolt was drawn, and the culprit, who had been given a drop of 7ft. 3in., died instantaneously. "There was not," said the chief gaol surgeon afterwards, "a quiver of the muscle after the body descended into the pit. Deceased was beyond pain instantly." "I think," said the Governor, at the inquest afterwards, "it is impossible to have performed the execution more skilfully. There was no hitch whatever. The sentence was duly carried out at eight o'clock exactly." The black emblem promptly at eight o'clock was run up the flagstaff, on the summit of the high towers, signalling the fate of Duckworth to the few knots of curious people who had been standing shivering on the outskirts of the prison in the cold gray dawn.

How the Preston Guardian told the tale of the Blackburn murderer

had brought the prisoner to that position, as it had brought many men before to the scaffold.

Concerning the jury's recommendation to mercy he assured the prisoner that his would be forwarded to the proper quarter.

As sentence of death was passed, Duckworth stood quite motionless and gave no indication that he felt the terrible position in which he had placed himself.

Finally, His Lordship addressed a question to the jury which was understood to be, whether the grounds of their recommendation to mercy were that the prisoner had not deliberately and intentionally murdered the child, but that her death had followed upon his attempts to stifle her cries during his assault upon her.

The Foreman replied that such was the case.

The date fixed for Cross Duckworth's execution was Tuesday, January the 3rd, 1893. All efforts to obtain a commutation of the sentence failed. An ultimatum from the Home Secretary that the law must take its course was read to him on the previous Saturday by the Governor of Walton Gaol.

Duckworth who had all along denied knowledge of the crime and had clung to the hope of a reprieve, based on the jury's recommendation to mercy, became terribly depressed. Nonetheless he slept fairly well during the remaining nights and appeared to eat his food with the usual relish.

On the Monday afternoon his wife, children and other relatives visited him and the farewell was a heart rendering one.

At a few minutes before eight o'clock on the Tuesday morning, the Governor of the gaol, the chaplain, the doctor and his assistant, the chief warder and a couple of other gaol officials formed an escort to accompany Duckworth on his journey to the scaffold. The condemned man, who had been pinioned by executioner James Billington, submitted to his fate like someone in a dream.

Punctually at eight o'clock the bolt was drawn, and the culprit, who had been given a drop of 7ft 3in died instantaneously. At once the black emblem was run up the flagstaff at the summit of the high towers and the fate of Duckworth was signalled to the small knot of curious people who had been standing shivering outside the prison on a cold grey morning.

Chapter 41

Two More upon The Scaffold

On Friday, May 16th 1862, William Galloway Mellor, who was a clerk employed by his father, Evan Mellor, was the first to arrive at their first floor business premises in South King Street, Manchester. A couple of minutes after his arrival William Taylor and his wife Martha entered the offices and enquired as to the whereabouts of his father. William told them his father was expected shortly and they both took a seat in the ante-room to await his arrival, with William Mellor returning to the inner office.

His father appeared some twelve minutes later and no sooner had he said "Good morning, Mr Taylor", than the visitor had sprung to his feet and grabbed Mr Mellor, senior, round the neck with his left-hand. Disturbed by the commotion, William Mellor rushed from the inner office to aid his father but was stopped in his tracks by Martha Taylor, who pointed a pistol at him. By this time his father and William Taylor were on the landing engaged in a fearful struggle. Fearing for his father's safety, William Mellor ran back into the inner office and throwing open a window, attempted to raise an alarm. As he did so, he heard the discharge of a pistol, to which he responded by dashing back through the ante-room on to the landing from where he saw his father lying on the lower landing. Some occupants of the building had rushed to his aid and he seemed in a critical condition, with blood flowing from his mouth and from his breast, with several cuts having been made in his waistcoat.

In his urgency to attend to his father, William Mellor must have rushed past Taylor because when he glanced upwards he saw his father's assailant on the upper landing, with a revolver in his hand, and looking down over the rail.

Leaving his father in the care of the onlookers he rushed out of the building to summon assistance from the nearby police station. As he did so he brushed past Mrs Taylor, who by now was standing on the ground floor. Within minutes, the police were on hand and William Taylor was taken into custody and the unfortunate Mr Mellor carried to the Infirmary. He was dead on arrival and his death was attributed to stab wounds to the chest and thigh. Upon their investigation the officers found a bloodstained knife in the ante-room of Mellor's office and a sheath, which the knife fitted, was found upon the person of William Taylor.

According to witnesses of the incident, who had been aroused by the sound of Mr Mellor falling down the stairs, they found him on the first floor landing, and as they went to his assistance they raised him to a sitting position. William Taylor made his way down the stairs and fired a pistol at Mr Mellor, the charge missed him and wounded one of the bystanders.

Further investigation showed that there had been a long running dispute between Mr Mellor and William Taylor, a provisions dealer. Mr Mellor had been the agent for a house and shop in Britannia Buildings, Strangeways, which Taylor and his family occupied. A boiler explosion had occurred on the premises in January of the same year and, as a result, one of Taylor's children was killed. Subsequently, he had wanted compensation for the damage and the loss of his child, and as a result refused to pay his rent. Mr Mellor arranged to have the premises repaired, but declined to offer any financial settlement.

The dispute had dragged on and become more complicated when Taylor had told Mellor that he was prepared to vacate the premises, with the understanding that they would forgo the outstanding rent. This was agreed, but no agreement could be reached over the value of the fixtures that Taylor was to leave behind. Eventually an enforcement order was taken out and through an appointed auctioneer, Taylor's goods were sold . This displeased Taylor who complained that his possessions had been sold under their value. Mr Mellor told him that his complaint should be made to the auctioneer, although Taylor in his mind felt he knew where the blame lay.

The tragic incident at Mr Mellor's business premises was only part of the charge to be laid on William Taylor's account. On the following Monday morning, both William Robert Taylor and his wife, Martha Ann Taylor, were brought up before a full bench of Magistrates in Manchester. Over the weekend, as the pair were taken into custody, a grim discovery had been made. Amidst great mystery, their three children had been found dead. Immediately it was suspected that they had been poisoned, but examinations by an analytical chemist brought a negative conclusion. Indeed, the surgeon into whose care the bodies of the children had been committed, told the gathering that at that stage neither he or other medical analysts had discovered how the youngsters came by their deaths.

Therefore the Magistrates concentrated their attention on the matter of the murder of Evan Mellor. Both William Taylor and his wife stood in the dock, the husband appearing to be in a considerable state of emotion, which he was struggling to repress and the wife, although looking pale, appeared to be more in control of her feelings. Mr Mellor's son was the chief witness and he gave a detailed account of the incident on the previous Friday morning, and explained to the court the origins of the long running argument between them.

The couple had no legal representative and chose to defend themselves, questioning the various witnesses when appropriate. At the conclusion of the hearing, Mr Maybery, the Chief Superintendent of Police, requested that the proceedings be adjourned and the prisoners remanded until further investigation had taken place.

That afternoon two funeral ceremonies took place. One paid for by public subscription was held for the three children and many hundreds of people assembled along the route to the Harpurhey cemetery. The funeral of Mr Mellor was a strictly private affair and none but family and immediate relatives and friends were invited, as he was conveyed from his house in Aldmonbury Place, Cornbrook to the parish church of Chorlton-cum-Hardy. He was laid to rest alongside his wife and the coffin plate and tombstone merely recorded the age of the deceased and the date of his death, no reference being made to the foul assassination.

When the inquest was resumed, some ten days later, there was still no satisfactory explanation for the deaths of the children. It was reported that chemical evidence showed there was no grounds to prove that an irritant or narcotic poison had been administered. The conclusion was that although they did not find poison it was probable that chloroform, applied in the form of vapour, had been used to bring to an end the lives of three apparently healthy children. There was however, enough evidence to commit the couple on the charge of murdering Evan Mellor and, on this offence, they were ordered to be tried at the forthcoming Liverpool Assizes.

When they appeared before Mr Baron Wilde at the Assizes, they were called upon to plead. The 37-year-old William Taylor answered by saying, "Not a shadow of guilt, my Lord", and his 25-year-old wife simply said, "Not guilty, my Lord".

Once again William Galloway Mellor had to repeat the evidence he had told the magistrates and relive his father's final moments. On this occasion both husband and wife had legal representatives, but the evidence against the husband appeared overwhelming.

His defence was one of insanity, while the wife's counsel suggested that although she had been present, she played no part in the killing, and that William Mellor, in his state of anxiety, had been mistaken when he suggested that she had in fact been in possession of the pistol. The Judge was dismissive to the plea of insanity, and pointed out to the Jury that the man had inflicted ten or twelve stab wounds and fired a pistol at his victim. It took the Jury just fifteen minutes to reach their verdicts, which were, "Guilty", against Taylor and, "Not Guilty", in respect of his wife. Mr Baron Wilde donned the black cap and addressing the prisoner informed him that he had been found guilty of a most barbarous murder, telling him, "You must have been aware, when you took that man's life, that you did so at the forfeit of your own!" He then passed the sentence of death in the usual form.

No sooner had the residents of the Manchester area got over the shock of the Taylor atrocities than another tragedy befell the neighbourhood. The newspapers, at the end of June, carried another shocking headline, announcing the murder of a policeman at Ashton-under-Lyne. On the last Saturday in June of that year, two members of the Lancashire Constabulary, Sergeant Harrop and Police Constable Jump were on duty at Smallshaw. About two o'clock that morning they came upon a band of seven or eight masked men, armed with pistols and bludgeons. They appeared to be brick makers, and the officers at once suspected that they had been engaged in the perpetration of some of the outrages from which the master brick makers of the district had suffered so severely.

They were in a field leading from Smallshaw Fold to Broad Oak Lane. The officers challenged them; a scuffle took place and two of the men were taken into custody. An appeal was made by one of the men, who asked his companions, "Do you mean to stand for this?". Jump immediately found himself in a desperate struggle with one of the men and received a severe blow on the back of his head. Sergeant Harrop succeeded in wrenching a bludgeon from one of the assailants and with this he defended himself. Soon a full blooded confrontation was taking place and the firing of a pistol aroused the residents of the tiny hamlet.

One woman, peering through her bedroom window, saw PC Jump intercepting one of the men who was attempting to escape through a stile. He threatened the officer with the words, "If you don't let me pass I will blow you to pieces". Within a minute both officers had been shot and their attackers were fleeing, some in the direction of Ashton-under-Lyne and others towards Wilshaw. Sergeant Harrop had been fired at first and the shot that struck him inflicted a wound over his right eye. However, his own injury was soon forgotten when he saw his colleague, slumped against a gate, crying in pain and dying from two bullet wounds, one in his left breast and the other in his back. Death was almost immediate and the body of PC Jump was conveyed to the head police station at Wilshaw. The constable was 29 years old and had entered the Lancashire Constabulary in September 1856, being stationed firstly at Droylsden.

The utmost excitement prevailed in Ashton when news of the constable's death was relayed and there was great sympathy for his widow and the five small children he left behind. The feeling was very strong that the perpetrators of the murder were union brick makers, as a short time before the killing 18,000 bricks had been destroyed in a brick yard near Stalybridge.

By midday, particulars of the murder had been discussed by the county Magistrates and a notice was posted, offering £200 for the apprehension and conviction of the murderers.

"£200 Reward-Murder-

Whereas, early this morning, Police Constable William Jump, and Sergeant George Harrop, were on duty at Smallshaw, in the parish of Ashton-under-Lyne, when they were met by seven or eight men, masked and armed with bludgeons and fire arms, one of whom fired two shots at and killed Police Constable Jump, and others of the party fired several shots at and wounded Police Sergeant Harrop. Notice is hereby given, that a reward of £100 will be paid by the magistrates of the county, and a further reward of £100 by Her Majesty's government, to any person giving such information and evidence as shall lead to the discovery and conviction of the murderer; and the Secretary of State has intimated that he will advise the grant of Her Majesty's gracious parden to any accomplice giving such information and evidence as shall lead to the same result. Information to be given to the chief constable of the county, at Preston; to Mr. King, the assistant chief constable, Bootle, near Liverpool; and to Mr. Lullain, superintendant of police, Wilshawe, Ashton-under-Lyne.-

By order of the magistrates.

"W.P. Egeo, chief constable of Lancashire.

Town Hall, Ashton-under-Lyne, June 29,1802"

When the hue and cry had subsided, five men stood trial for the killing of the constable. Of the five, two men, Michael Burke an Irishman and a Catholic, and Ward an Englishman and a Protestant, were condemned to die. The scene of the murder had been painstakingly searched by the police and among the incriminating evidence was a screwed up piece of paper which belonged to one of those arrested, and unfired clay bricks bearing marks matching the boots of the accused.

As a result, William Calcraft was engaged to visit Kirkdale Gaol to carry out the executions of Burke, Ward and William Robert Taylor, the Manchester murderer. Representatives of both Burke and Ward were busy making urgent appeals for the commutation of the sentence passed upon them. At first these exertions were apparently unheeded, and then on the Friday night before the Saturday executions, as Burke was making his final farewell, in his cell with his wife, a telegram was received by Captain Gibb, the Governor of the gaol. It informed the official that Burke's execution was not to take place and that a respite would follow. The news was conveyed by the prison chaplain and husband and wife embraced each other in unabridged joy. Eventually Burke was to suffer transportation for his crime, but to escape the clutches of Calcraft left him temporarily overjoyed.

Ward, who expressed contrition for his offences, was painfully depressed during his final days and when he heard of Burke's reprieve, was very much dispirited. He was left to share the scaffold with Taylor, whose notoriety had grown during the five months since his atrocious crime.

Taylor's reputation went before him. The only son of a Somerset tea dealer he was, as a youth, apprenticed to a shoemaker. Then he filled a number of occupations, including school teacher, commercial clerk and traveller. Still a young man he connected himself to a body of professing Christians, and threw himself into active public life amongst them. In 1849, he had married his first wife, but, in less than ten years she had died, leaving him with four young children. In 1861, he had taken his second wife who was a young woman, respectably connected. What followed was a catalogue of forgery, disgrace, misfortune, blind passion, insatiable revenge and foul murder, following each other in rapid succession, leaving him to pay the ultimate penalty in a hardened and unforgiving state.

Throughout his confinement, Taylor daily wrote to his wife, expressing his devotion to her in language bordering on the romantic.

During his imprisonment, he stated that neither chloroform nor wet towels caused the death of his children and that it was nothing but simple medicine that he used, and he expressed his surprise at the medical experts' failure to detect his methods.

Soon after eight o'clock on the Saturday morning the streets leading to Kirkdale were thronged with people wending their way slowly towards the centre of attraction. At noon the spectators numbered close on 120,000. Information had been received a few days previous, that the brick makers intended to come to the executions in a body, with the object of assaulting Calcraft. The rumour proved to be unfounded, although every precaution was taken to meet the emergency should it arise, with in excess of two hundred constables being employed in the vicinity of the gallows.

Shortly after twelve o'clock, Taylor and Ward appeared on the scaffold with various officials. Taylor glanced around the multitude with a strange, calm expression and Ward, equally calm, took up his position to Taylor's right and, as he did so, he threw his cap into the crowd in a determined manner.

Both men appeared in good health and both wore the clothes that they were dressed in at their respective trials. Calcraft, having pinioned their legs, proceeded to draw their caps over their faces. There was a slight murmur in the crowd and the people evidently expecting a speech from Taylor shouted his name. Taylor, who had stated he regretted murdering Mr Mellor, but not the children, had, on several occasions intimated his intention to make a speech on the gallows. However, he was dissuaded by gaol officials during the final hours.

Acknowledging the crowd, Taylor gracefully bowed three times and then quietly addressed one of the gaol officials. The chaplain recited the appropriate verses and Ward, with a tone of touching earnestness, repeated them.

Calcraft then shook hands with both men and retired from the platform. In less than five minutes from their arrival on the scaffold, the drop fell, and all was over.

The press representatives were then admitted to the gaol and were met by the Governor, Captain Gibb. It was stated that Taylor had refused to reveal the cause of the childrens' death, replying to the request with the words, "I will take it with me". In reply to a question of whether the children had suffered much, he had merely stated that they were dead eight days before the murder of Mellor. On the morning of his execution Taylor had received a letter from his wife, begging that he would send her a silk pocket handkerchief and, on the scaffold, he had asked the prison chaplain if he would kindly forward it to her.

The executions had been witnessed by a great cross-section of the community. Ladies in crinoline, bare-footed youths, young mothers with babes in arms, gentlemen and beggars – many at the scene had walked forty miles, and would have to walk it back again.

Chapter 42

Murder and then Mutilation

In the middle of May 1891, detectives in Liverpool were busy at work attempting to discover the perpetrator of the terrible murder of a boy called Nicholas Martin. The mutilated body of the ten-year-old had been found in a bag floating in the Sandon Dock. The corpse with its throat cut, was wrapped in a blanket, fully dressed except for cap and boots, and the clothing was not disarranged. The legs had been cut off at the knees in order that the body would fit in the bag, which also contained a saw and a knife, both of which bore evidence of having been used to mutilate the body. In the boy's pocket were found a sixpence and a penny.

The victim was described as a big fine lad who looked older than his years. He was the youngest of the eleven children that made up the Martin family. His father being a respectable man with over twenty years service at the Keeling and Company Soap Works where he was a foreman.

The family home was in Bridgewater Street and according to the boy's parents the youngster was an obedient son, who regularly attended school and was never in the habit of straying from home or wandering about the docks.

On the day of his disappearance, Saturday the 16th of May, at about seven o'clock in the evening, his father had given him a penny and sent him off to play. A couple of hours later, whilst out shopping, his mother saw him and told him to go home. He had then turned in that direction and that was the last she saw of him alive.

When he did not turn up at home the parents informed the police and later reading of the find at Sandon Dock, they feared that it could be their child. Their worst fears were realised when they viewed the mutilated remains.

The early police enquiries were concentrated on boarding houses in the neighbourhood of the docks, in the belief that the crime had been the work of a seafaring man. The parents identification of the boy had taken place on the Tuesday and the search was switched to the areas in which he might have been playing.

Diligent investigations eventually led to suspicion falling on John Conway, the secretary and delegate of the Seaman and Firemen's Union, who occupied premises for his Union activities in Stanhope Street. Senior police officers visited the building which consisted of three rooms, one of which was used as an office. The place appeared to have been recently swept. In the oven were two bundles of chips, some brown paper and a partly torn label. The brown paper and label being similar to one's found in the bag in which the body had been placed. On the floor of the topmost room there was a large patch with streaks of red in it.

Within hours Conway was arrested at his lodgings in Bridgewater Street and when interviewed in the detective office he was told that a woman had identified him as the man who purchased the bag and the blanket from her shop. By the Friday there was enough evidence to convince the police that Conway was the killer and he was accordingly charged with murder. In reply he said, "My God, My God, I am not Guilty".

The trial of 60-year-old John Conway, described as a marine fireman, took place at Liverpool Assizes before Mr Justice Smith. Great interest was created and the venue, St. George's Hall, was beset by a crowd of people anxious to get into court. All were curious to view the trial of a man who some years before had lodged with the Martin family at their Bridgewater Street home.

Two of the witnesses called stated that they had seen the prisoner leave his office on the Monday with a heavy bag. He had driven away in a cab, and a cabman spoke as to having taken the accused to the Landing Stage of the docks. The prisoner's landlady and other lodgers described his movements over the tragic period and how he had drunk a great deal and been in an excitable state.

Another witness identified Conway as the man he had seen giving sixpence to the murdered boy on the Saturday night and as being the person the boy had gone away with.

The trial took the best part of two days and Conway's defence revolved around a statement that he had purchased the bag and blankets for a foreign sailor who wished to join the Union. This sailor had, he claimed, left the bag at the Union office and asked Conway to take it to the pier-head if he did not return for it.

Conway's version of events gained little credibility with the Jury who spent only twenty minutes finding him Guilty. Mr Justice Smith at once sentencing him to death.

James Berry, public hangman 1884-1892 - was in a hurry to despatch the killer into eternity.

The date set for the execution was Thursday, August 20th 1891, the venue being Kirkdale Gaol, Liverpool. During the preceding night the culprit slept fairly well, awaking at five o'clock in the morning and afterwards attending Mass and receiving the last Sacrament at the hands of the Roman Catholic chaplain.

James Berry, the executioner, entered the pinioning room a few minutes before eight o'clock and after he had adjusted the straps the procession moved to the execution room. Conway looked dazed and scared, but he walked firmly to the scaffold. After being placed on the drop, and as Berry was about to place the white cap over his head, the condemned man asked if he could speak. Berry was anxious to get on with his task but the chaplain intervened and Conway turned to those present and addressed them. He urged them to beware of drink, which had been his ruin and he spoke of the kindness with which he had been treated while in gaol. He also expressed the hope that the boy's parents would forgive him.

Berry then placed the cap over Conway's head, adjusted the rope and pulled the lever. The culprit dropped and immediately a curious sound like rushing water was heard, and when those present looked down into the pit they were horrified to see that the man's head had been almost torn off, and blood was pouring down. The sight was sickening to the witnesses and reporters gathered and they were at once ordered away from the place by the governor of the gaol, Major Knox. They were only too willing to depart as they had witnessed a scene they would never forget.

Later the executioner met the reporters in the Warders' Room and one of them said, "You've made a mess of it this time, Mr Berry". To which the hangman replied, "Not I, I am not to blame for anything that has occurred. All is left to the doctor now, and this comes of not taking my advice. They would have given him another eight inches drop but for me". The reporter then asked whether the drop was fixed by new Government Regulations and Berry replied, "Yes, that is right enough; but this is the fruits of interfering with my decision. But for me they would have decapitated him altogether".

Berry seemed anxious that the reporters should say nothing about the matter and at the inquest it was stated that there had been no hitch in the execution. Death had obviously been instantaneous not only due to the fracture of the neck, but also the bursting of the blood vessels. Viewed from the brink of the scaffold, the rope had bitten deep into Conway's neck and his flesh seemed to have given way like a rotten garment under the sudden strain.

The executioner left the gaol as soon as he could and appeared less collected than usual as he hurried away to his home in Bradford. He had been greatly upset by the shocking spectacle and early that evening when reporters gathered at his house, they were told he had gone to bed, with instructions not to be disturbed.

From the gaol came news that Conway had requested that reporters be informed of his full confession. He had expressed penitence and offered his life in atonement of the crime. With regard to the disposal of the boy's body, he had stated "I went on board a Woodside ferryboat, and at about ten o'clock at night, when we were in mid river I dropped the canvas bag overboard, but knew not where it went. I thought it would be carried out to sea."

Ironically, the Liverpool Dock murderer's despatch into eternity had been as horrible as the crime he had committed.

Chapter 43

An Able Seaman's Awful End

In May 1857, the "Martha Jane", a bark owned at Sunderland, set off on her homeward voyage from Barbados to Liverpool. Aboard the vessel was an able seaman by the name of Andrew Rose. The voyage under the Captain, Henry Rogers, aged 35, First Mate William Miles, aged 27 and Second Mate, Charles Edward Seymour, aged 25, was to be the last one he would make.

The ship arrived at Liverpool on the 9th of June and when it docked information soon leaked of the awful end of Andrew Rose.

He had been singled our for special treatment owing to the fact that he had fled the vessel prior to sailing, having been negligent in his duties. The local police had returned him to the captain's charge just hours before they left Barbados. From that day he was subjected to a series of barbarities which had no parallel in the annals of brutality. He was repeatedly beaten with a rope and heavy whip and put in irons; gagged with an iron bolt thrust into his mouth, and fastened with a rope carried round his head; torn by a dog that was set upon him by the captain, until blood came; sent up aloft naked, followed by the Chief Mate with a whip, which was applied to his bare limbs; had his own excrement forced into his mouth and nostrils; was fastened in a water-cask and rolled about the deck, without any means of getting air except through the bung hole; was kept there without food or water for hours and was finally run up to the yard-arm, where he remained suspended by the neck until he was black in the face, his eyes protruding, his tongue lolled out, and froth coming from his mouth; and when cut down he fell flat as if dead. A day or two after this, on or about the 5th June, he died.

He had wounds all over his body from the beatings and cruelties he had suffered. His wounds had festered and he was in such a state that the crew were loth to touch him. They dragged him aft with a rope and, in about an hour afterwards, by order of Captain Rogers, he was thrown overboard.

Consequently, Henry Rogers, William Miles and Charles Seymour were charged with murder on the high seas. The three prisoners were all found Guilty at the trial, on the 19th of August, before Mr Baron

Watson. His Lordship had no alternative but to sentence all three to be executed for their ill-usage of the unfortunate Rose.

Great exertions were made by Mr Snowball, the solicitor for the prisoners, and some philanthropic gentlemen, with a view of inducing the Home Secretary to spare the lives of the condemned men. The early efforts were unattended with even the least measure of success. Eventually, in the final week before the execution date, Mr Snowball managed to obtain an interview with Sir George Grey, the Home Secretary. Before him he urged all the circumstances most favourable to the prisoners, including the claim that none of them had struck Rose for several days before his death, whereas the trial had shown that the cook knocked him against the gangway the day before he died. Mr Snowball also urged that the seaman Groves, one of the main trial witnesses, was unworthy of belief.

As things transpired the solicitors efforts were more successful than those previously made because on the Wednesday morning the governor of the gaol at Kirkdale received a communication from the Home Secretary. It was to the effect that Sir George Grey saw no reason why the law should not take its usual course with regard to Captain Henry Rogers, but that the two men condemned with him would have their lives spared and their sentence commuted to penal servitude for life.

Up to this period the Captain and the Mates had occupied the same cell, but after breaking the news, it was necessary to part them.

The painful task of relaying the intelligence was done by the chaplain of the gaol, the Rev Richard Appleton, who had been unremitting in his attention to them. The Mates were quite unmanned, and wept bitterly, either from excess of joy at their own deliverance from an ignominious death, or from grief at the approaching fate of their Commander, to whom they had been evidently closely attached.

Captain Rogers received the intelligence with firmness, unmarked by bravado – the firmness of a man who was prepared to die, having made his peace with his creator. Before the separation they requested that they might be allowed an hour together for prayer, a boon which was granted to them, and they united in devotion for a prolonged period. The Mates were then removed to another cell, and a turnkey was placed in constant attendance upon Captain Rogers.

The most distressing feature of the case lay in the fact that the condemned criminal had a wife and five children. The two eldest, a fine lad of fourteen and a good looking girl of twelve, having along with their mother had several interviews with the unhappy man during his final week. The boy, who was present at the trial, seemed to feel acutely the dreadful position in which his father stood. The little girl seemed unconscious of his approaching end, although he told her at their final meeting on the Friday, that she would never see him again on earth.

At that interview the scene was pathetic beyond description, but the poignancy of the grief was subdued by the consolations of religion, in which the afflicted wife seemed specially to seek refuge in her distress. She was a member of the Wesleyan body and had from time to time urged her husband to place his trust and hope in the Saviour. Before their separation, Captain Rogers expressed a wish that his wife should be present while the chaplain offered up a prayer.

William Calcraft, the executioner, arrived on the Friday evening and slept the night at the gaol. Saturday morning, the 12th of September, ushered in a clear, sunny day, the brightness and warmth of which presented a remarkable contrast to the wet, cold and miserable weather of the preceding day.

At an early hour the scaffold was projected from the north west corner of the gaol, at a point commanding an uninterrupted view of the Channel and the docks, crowded with large fleets of merchantmen of all nations. Crowds soon thronged the thoroughfares leading to the place of execution and omnibuses transported the shop-keeping classes whilst lorries and donkey carts were filled with dock porters and basket women. Among the masses were women with babes in arms, and lads with shoe-less feet and scanty clothing. Thus the crowd continued to increase until it was computed that not less than 50,000 persons were present.

At twelve o'clock an awful stillness hung over the great multitude as the procession made its appearance on the scaffold. First came the culprit, dressed in black, with his neck bared and his arms pinioned. He was accompanied by Calcraft, the hangman, a portly man, also dressed in black, and with a gold watch-chain displayed across his breast. They were followed by Mr Birchall the deputy Sheriff, Captain Gibb, the governor of the jail and Mr Wright, the prison philantropist, who had arrived the previous day, and who had that morning spent some time in prayer with the culprit.

Captain Rogers moved forward with a firm step, pausing for a moment as if awed by the light of those fifty thousand upturned faces

Andrew Rose, the British sailor
Now to you his woes I'll name-
'Twas on the passage from Barbadoes
Whilst on board of the "Martha Jane".

(Chorus) Wasn't that most cruel usage,
Without a friend to interpose?
How they whipped and mangled, gagged and strangled
The British sailor, Andrew Rose.

'Twas on the quarter-deck they laid him,
Gagged him with an iron bar;
Wasn't that most cruel usage
To put upon a British tar?

'Twas up aloft the captain sent him,
Naked beneath the burning sun,
Whilst the mate did follow after,
Lashing him till the blood did run.

The captain gave him stuff to swallow;
Stuff to you I will not name,
Whilst the crew got sick with horror,
While on board the "Martha Jane".

'Twas in a water-cask they put him;
Seven long days they kept him there.
When loud for mercy Rose did venture,
The captain swore no man should go there.

For twenty days they did ill-use him,
When into Liverpool they arrived.
The judge he heard young Andrew's story;
"Captain Rogers, you must die".

Come all ye friends and near relations.
And all ye friends to interpose;
Never treat a British sailor
Like they did young Andrew Rose.

– himself the one chief object of attention. Withdrawing his eyes from the multitude, he glanced towards the sea on which he had spent 25 years of his life, and appeared for a moment to look tenderly towards the tall masts which rose skyward from the docks along the margin of the river. Firmly still, but without bravado, he stepped forward and placed himself under the drop, where Calcraft adjusted the rope and prepared to place the cap over the culprit's face.

Before this was accomplished, Rogers addressed some earnest words to the executioner, who seemed not to understand him. The chaplain, who had in the meantime proceeded with the service, moved forward, a few words were exchanged between him and the culprit, who then shook hands with Calcraft, and in a moment more all was over.

After the body had been suspended for the usual time, it was cut down and buried within the precincts of the jail. The multitude began to disperse immediately the bolt was drawn, and in an hour few of that vast concourse of people remained in front of the scaffold.

Captain Rogers made no proper confession of his guilt. He did not deny the ill-usage of the tragic able seaman; but in a style worthy of a special pleader, he told the chaplain a few moments before his death, that he wished it to be understood that he had done nothing to cause the death of Andrew Rose.

At the time of the execution the "Martha Jane", a handy bark of 350 tons on which the barbarities had occurred, was lying in the Wapping Dock, Liverpool.

There was a certain amount of sympathy for Captain Rogers and a subscription was set on foot for his widow which realised about seven hundred pounds.

Postscript: Within days of the execution a model of Captain Rogers was placed in the Chamber of Horrors waxworks in Liverpool. The clothes it was draped in had been purchased from executioner Calcraft, and were the actual clothes worn on the scaffold by the barbarous sea captain.

Chapter 44

Shooting of HM Customs' Officer

In 1832, William Southgate arrived at Liverpool as an Inspector of Customs, having previously been occupied in the Excise department. Shortly after his arrival, Mr Southgate had occasion to report Norman Welch, who was employed as a locker by His Majesty's Customs. Welch, who had spent fifteen years employed at Liverpool, was accused after thirteen pieces of calico had gone missing from the warehouse in which he was employed. He claimed he knew nothing about the missing goods but, as a result of the report, he was downgraded to the position of weigher. It was an employment inferior in both importance and emolument, which in cash terms meant a reduction of £20 per year in earnings.

As time passed, Welch brooded on his situation and felt that Mr Southgate only spoke to him to find fault. On one occasion he had been seen eating his dinner on a cask in the warehouse and his superior had told him that was not the place to dine. At other times Mr Southgate indicated his distaste with Welch's drinking habits and it was common knowledge that he was drinking a great deal.

The taking of spirits seemed to keep Welch's mind in constant agitation and his dislike for Southgate increased with each passing day. Eventually, in the middle of October 1834, he went to a shop in Liverpool and purchased a pistol, saying he had a wager with a friend and wanted a pistol for the purpose of deciding it. He was given instructions as to the mode of loading and firing it and purchased some percussion caps for it.

A couple of days later on Friday, October 17th, Mr Southgate was standing outside the Custom House, in conversation with a man named Pike, when almost from nowhere Norman Welch appeared brushing past Pike and confronting a startled Mr Southgate. He drew from his right-hand coat pocket a pistol and, as Mr Southgate drew back and raised his arms, Welch pressed the trigger and shot him in the lower rib cage.

As Mr Southgate slumped to the ground he cried out, "I am shot – I am shot", and Welch dropped the pistol to the floor. As the victim was taken into a nearby building, Welch was grabbed by a couple of

In 1834 The Liverpool Custom House was the scene of William Southgate's murder

bystanders who asked, "Who has done this?", to which he replied, "It was me – a robbed man".

Mr Southgate was subsequently removed to his own house, where he died the following Sunday afternoon. The fatal wound was under the seventh rib on the left-hand side of his chest and death was due to the laceration of the stomach by the passage of the ball.

After Welch had been secured he was asked whether he realised what he had done, to which he replied, "Yes. I have shot a damn rogue who has robbed me". When examined, there was found upon his body a quantity of laudanum, which was strung in a bottle around his waist. When asked about the laudanum he stated that he did not intend to destroy himself, but merely take a few drops to make him sleep.

The following March, Norman Welch appeared at Lancaster Assizes before Mr Baron Parke, charged with the wilful murder of Mr Southgate. The main hope for Welch revolved around his mental condition and various employees of the Customs department, and other acquaintances, gave evidence that they considered him not of sound mind when in a state of excitement.

It was also recalled how, many years before while quartered in Ireland with the 2nd Lancashire Militia, he had got into a row and been very seriously beaten. He was in hospital for a long time and since then he had claimed that liquor had affected him very much.

However, medical experts who had interviewed him after the tragic shooting, were of the opinion that he showed no signs of insanity during their discussions.

When His Lordship summed up the trial proceedings he stated that there was no doubt as to the fact that the deceased met his end at the hands of the prisoner. He then went into the question of the state of the prisoner's mind and discussed the wealth of evidence that had been presented. He observed that the act was not inconsistent with the diabolical passion of revenge, but remarked that it was not every frantic fit of passion that should be deemed insanity.

In all the summing up occupied two hours, and the jury, after a few minutes consultation, found the prisoner Guilty.

The judge then put on the black cap and sentenced the prisoner to be hanged on the following Monday and his body to be buried within the precincts of the prison, according to the forms of the Statute. His Lordship suggested Welch spend the remaining hours of his life in diligent prayer and entreaty that might be acceptable to God. The prisoner descended the steps of the dock with a firm step.

Heeding the advice of His Lordship he spent the little time afforded to him in religious exercises and preparation for the awful end that awaited him. He was said to have acknowledged the justice of his sentence and expressed the greatest contrition for his crime.

On the Saturday he was visited by his eldest son and his brother-in-law and on the Sunday he attended Divine Service in the chapel of the gaol.

When Monday morning arrived some thousand plus persons had gathered to witness the end of the 56-year-old who was prepared to leave behind his wife and six children. As the Lancaster Castle clock struck eight he was led on to the scaffold, exhibiting the utmost firmness. The adjustment of the rope, a bow to the gathered assembly, a moment of prayer, the drawing of the bolt and Norman Welch was launched into eternity.

Chapter 45

A Cry of Innocence Ignored

On the morning of the 22nd July in 1889, the murder took place of a man by the name of Walter Davies. The scene of the crime was a jeweller's shop in Atherton, near Manchester where Davies had been employed as a shop man for ten weeks. The premises were owned by a Mr John Lowe who carried on business as a watch-maker and pawnbroker with outlets in various districts of Manchester.

On the day of his death, Davies went to his employers home to receive his instructions and to collect a quantity of articles for display in the Atherton shop. By eight o'clock he had arrived at the premises and shortly afterwards was seen by a local woman hanging watches in the front window.

About half an hour later the woman, Jane Clowers, went into the shop and called out for Mr Davies. Receiving no reply to her call she left the premises only to return a few minutes afterwards. On the second occasion when she again received no reply to her shout, she became somewhat anxious. Her concerns heightening when she became alerted by a choking noise coming from the cellar.

Fearful of what lay in store behind the cellar door, she returned to her nearby home and persuaded her husband and son to accompany her back to the jeweller's shop . Upon their entry to the shop all was quiet and they at once made their way to the cellar. As soon as they opened the door and began to descend the cellar steps they found Walter Davies lying almost on his back near the water tap. Large pools of blood led from the bottom of the steps to the spot where the man was lying.

The police were at once alerted and medical assistance was soon on hand. It was too late to revive the unfortunate man and it was observed that there was a bruise under each ear and a wound on one side of his temple.

On close examination of the premises by Mr Lowe it was realised that a quantity of watches, ornaments and wearing apparel was missing. Plunder had apparently been the intent of the visitor and the intruder's observation by Davies had led to the killing.

William Chadwick, 28 year old labourer, charged with murder

Intense investigations were set on foot and eventually a man called John Edward Lorne was charged with the murder. He had been positively identified as having visited a couple of pawnbrokers with watches, believed to have been from the stolen bounty. However, within three weeks it was realised that Lorne was not the man and he was released from custody.

The matter remained very high on the list of priorities and in October the police obtained the breakthrough they desired when William Chadwick, a 28-year-old labourer, was placed on remand at Strangeway's Gaol accused of committing a number of robberies on the railway.

Whilst in custody Chadwick was found to have in his possession five pawn tickets and it was arranged that the prisoner and a police officer would go to the pawnshops concerned to redeem the articles on pawn. Their visits led to the recovery of a lady's travelling bag containing a coat, a vest and four pairs of trousers, similar to those which had been taken from Mr Lowe's shop. Also inside the travelling bag was found a small handbag which contained seven silk handkerchiefs, reckoned to be part of the haul from the jeweller's shop.

The evidence against Chadwick was mounting and within days he was charged with the murder of Walter Davies. In reply he said, "I'm not guilty, and I am not going to plead guilty". His claim of innocence was repeated at the opening of his trial at the Liverpool Assizes towards the end of March 1890. The presiding Judge was Sir J.C. Matthew and he remarked that the evidence against the accused was for the most part circumstantial.

Various items of the stolen jewellery had been pawned and conflicting evidence was given by various pawnbrokers as to the identity of the person who had pledged the items. There was confusion over the appearance of Chadwick and a hairdresser from Eccles told the court that Chadwick had been supplied by him with a bottle of mixture to darken his hair, which had been lighter than his moustache, which he at the time wore.

Concerning a gold watch pawned in Manchester just hours after the killing, one pawnbroker stated that he was absolutely certain that Chadwick was the man who had pawned the item.

Various witnesses were called to testify that they had see Chadwick on the morning of the murder. A knocker up claimed he had seen him heading in the direction of Atherton and a colliery engine-man recalled seeing him just after six o'clock that morning in Leigh Lane, Atherton. Another man was positive that he has seen Chadwick beside the Punch Bowl Mill in Atherton, remembering in particular that the man he saw had a mutilated second finger on his right-hand. It was a fact that part of Chadwick's finger was missing and this had been noticed when Chadwick requested some matches off him.

One notable witness called by the defence was Detective Inspector Caminada, one of Manchester's leading criminal investigators. He was questioned relative to the earlier arrest of Lorne and he was asked about the positive identification of that man by two of the pawnbrokers.

In all the trial lasted three days and when the succession of eye witnesses, pawnbrokers and police officers had delivered their evi-

Detective Inspector Caminada was called to give evidence

dence the prosecution and the defence Counsel attempted to persuade the jury of Chadwick's innocence or guilt.

The prosecution appeared confident that they had provided enough evidence to link the prisoner to the robbery and the subsequent murder. They also attempted to make light of the fact that Lorne had been identified previously by men who now swore to the positive identification of Chadwick.

The defence Counsel suggested that the police had been over zealous in their search for the truth and remarked that the evidence presented was purely circumstantial. He also called into question the value of the evidence by the pawnbrokers who after being prepared to condemn Lorne, now suggested that Chadwick was the guilty man.

He then commented on the fact that the doctor who examined the victim had said that the murderer must have bloodstains upon his clothing – yet not a single bloodstained garment had been produced.

His claim was that his client's character was that of a thief and a receiver of stolen goods and that it was the custom amongst men of his class for stolen property to be passed on for pawning. He concluded by asking the jury to believe that such was the course that had led to his client's place in the dock.

The jury retired shortly after two o'clock and returned into court some forty minutes later, with a verdict of Guilty. Following the verdict the clerk of the Assizes asked the prisoner if he had anything to say prior to sentencing. He responded by making a long statement in which he protested that he had been the victim of a conspiracy. The lengthy address included the following: "I am innocent of this charge. I will say it now and I will say it on the scaffold. I am not afraid to die. All I want is justice and I have not had it".

His Lordship then reminded Chadwick that he had been found guilty of murder and proceeded to pass the sentence of death in the usual form.

The prisoner then made a further attempt to speak, but was quickly removed from the dock shouting out, "Goodbye, Polly", in reference to his wife, as he descended the steps.

The execution of William Chadwick took place on Tuesday, April 15th, 1890 and the task was performed by James Berry. At the subsequent inquest it was reported that death had been instantaneous – the statistics recorded that Chadwick, who was 5ft 5½inches tall and weighted 133½ lbs. had been given a drop of 8ft 2½inches.

It was reported that he had made no final statement and that his last words had been, "God Bless you all".

On the following day a letter appeared in the local newspapers and it had been written by Chadwick to his wife. In it were the following words:

> I have other things to confess, but thank God I am innocent of this murder. You were the wife of a dishonest man, but not the wife of a murderer. I freely forgive those led astray to swear me guilty.
>
> God bless, dear wife,
>
> I hope we shall meet in heaven above.
>
> Your unhappy husband,
>
> William

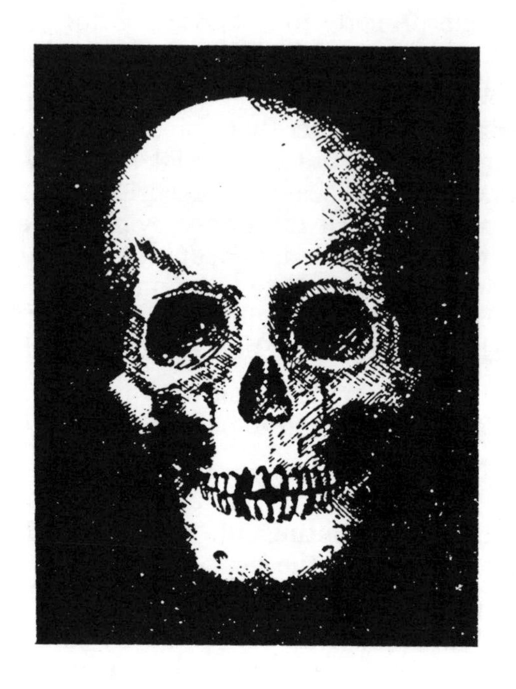

THE END

More books on Northern England folklore & heritage:

SHADOWS: A NORTHERN INVESTIGATION OF THE UNKNOWN – Steve Cliffe *(£7.95)*

DARK TALES OF OLD CHESHIRE – Angela Conway *(£6.95)*

CHESHIRE: ITS MAGIC & MYSTERY – Doug Pickford *(£7.95)*

MYTHS AND LEGENDS OF EAST CHESHIRE – Doug Pickford *(£5.95)*

GHOSTS, TRADITIONS & LEGENDS OF LANCASHIRE – Ken Howarth *(£7.95)*

SUPERNATURAL STOCKPORT – Martin Mills *(£5.95)*

JOURNEY THROUGH LANCASHIRE – Kenneth Fields *(£7.95)*

OLD NOTTINGHAMSHIRE REMEMBERED – Keith Taylor *(£7.95)*

STRANGE SOUTH YORKSHIRE – David Clarke *(£6.95)*

TRADITIONAL PUBS OF OLD LANCASHIRE – Peter Barnes *(£7.95)*

GOLDEN DAYS: A Macclesfield Life – Paul Maybury *(£6.95)*

MACCLESFIELD IN PICTURES & POEMS – Dorothy Bentley Smith *(£6.95)*

PORTRAIT OF MACCLESFIELD – Doug Pickford *(£6.95)*

MACCLESFIELD SO WELL REMEMBERED – Doug Pickford *(£6.95)*

MACCLESFIELD, THOSE WERE THE DAYS – Doug Pickford *(£6.95)*

PORTRAIT OF WILMSLOW – Ron Lee *(£7.95)*

PORTRAIT OF STOCKPORT – John Creighton *(£6.95)*

PORTRAIT OF MANCHESTER – John Creighton *(£6.95)*

PORTRAIT OF WARRINGTON – Jen Darling *(£6.95)*

Country Walking:

SECRET YORK: WALKS WITHIN THE CITY WALLS – Les Pierce *(£6.95)*

PUB WALKS IN THE YORKSHIRE DALES – Clive Price *(£6.95)*

PUB WALKS ON THE NORTH YORK MOORS & COAST – Stephen Rickerby *(£6.95)*

PUB WALKS IN THE YORKSHIRE WOLDS – Tony Whittaker *(£6.95)*

BEST PUB WALKS IN & AROUND SHEFFIELD – Clive Price *(£6.95)*

BEST PUB WALKS IN SOUTH YORKSHIRE – Martin Smith *(£6.95)*

THE LAKELAND SUMMITS – Tim Synge *(£7.95)*

100 LAKE DISTRICT HILL WALKS – Gordon Brown *(£7.95)*

LAKELAND ROCKY RAMBLES: Geology beneath your feet – Brian Lynas *(£7.95)*

FULL DAYS ON THE FELLS: Challenging Walks – Adrian Dixon *(£7.95)*

PUB WALKS IN THE LAKE DISTRICT – Neil Coates *(£6.95)*

YORKSHIRE DALES WALKING: ON THE LEVEL – Norman Buckley *(£6.95)*

LAKELAND WALKING, ON THE LEVEL – Norman Buckley *(£6.95)*

STROLLING WITH STEAM : walks along the Keswick Railway – Jan Darrall *(£4.95)*

TEA SHOP WALKS IN THE LAKE DISTRICT – Jean Patefield *(£6.95)*

MOSTLY DOWNHILL: LEISURELY WALKS, LAKE DISTRICT – Alan Pears *(£6.95)*

MOSTLY DOWNHILL IN THE PEAK DISTRICT – Clive Price *(£6.95)*
(two volumes, White Peak & Dark Peak)

EAST CHESHIRE WALKS – Graham Beech *(£5.95)*

WEST CHESHIRE WALKS – Jen Darling *(£5.95)*

WELSH WALKS: Dolgellau /Cambrian Coast – L. Main & M. Perrott *(£5.95)*

WELSH WALKS: Aberystwyth & District – L. Main & M. Perrott *(£5.95)*

WALKS IN MYSTERIOUS WALES – Laurence Main *(£7.95)*

RAMBLES IN NORTH WALES – Roger Redfern *(£6.95)*

PUB WALKS IN SNOWDONIA – Laurence Main *(£6.95)*

RAMBLES AROUND MANCHESTER – Mike Cresswell *(£5.95)*

FIFTY CLASSIC WALKS IN THE PENNINES – Terry Marsh *(£8.95)*

River and Canal Walks

PEAKLAND RIVER VALLEY WALKS – Tony Stephens

NORTH COUNTRY RIVER VALLEY WALKS – due Spring 1997 – Tony Stephens

WATERWAY WALKS AROUND BIRMINGHAM – David Perrott

WATERWAY WALKS IN LEICESTERSHIRE & RUTLAND – Paul Biggs

NORTH-WEST WATERWAY WALKS: NORTH OF THE MERSEY – Dennis Needham

NORTH-WEST WATERWAY WALKS: SOUTH OF THE MERSEY – Guy Lawson

NORTH -WEST WATERWAY WALKS: THE MERSEY WATERWAYS – David Parry

. . . all at £6.95

Cycling . . .

CYCLE UK! The essential guide to leisure cycling – Les Lumsdon *(£9.95)*

OFF-BEAT CYCLING IN THE PEAK DISTRICT – Clive Smith *(£6.95)*

MORE OFF-BEAT CYCLING IN THE PEAK DISTRICT – Clive Smith *(£6.95)*

CYCLING IN THE LAKE DISTRICT – John Wood *(£7.95)*

50 BEST CYCLE RIDES IN CHESHIRE – Graham Beech *(£7.95)*

CYCLING IN NOTTINGHAMSHIRE – Penny & Bill Howe *(£7.95)*

CYCLING IN SCOTLAND & N.E. ENGLAND – Philip Routledge *(£7.95)*

CYCLING IN NORTH WALES – Philip Routledge *(£7.95)*

CYCLING IN & AROUND BIRMINGHAM – Philip Routledge *(£7.95)*

CYCLING IN & AROUND MANCHESTER – Les Lumsdon*(£7.95)*